mindfulness
for teen anxiety

a workbook for overcoming anxiety at home, at school & everywhere else

CHRISTOPHER WILLARD, PsyD

Instant Help Books
An Imprint of New Harbinger Publications, Inc.

Publisher's Note

"Thoughts on Parade" adapted from "Thought Parade Exercise" in ACCEPTANCE AND MINDFULNESS TREATMENTS FOR CHILDREN AND ADOLESCENTS by Laurie A. Greco and Steven C. Hayes. Copyright © 2008 by Laurie A. Greco and Steven C. Hayes. Used by permission of New Harbinger Publications.

"The Guest House" from THE ESSENTIAL RUMI by Jalal al-Din Rumi, translated by Coleman Barks. Translation copyright © 1997 by Coleman Barks. Used by permission of Coleman Barks.

"Go Among Trees" copyright © 1998 by Wendell Berry from A TIMBERED CHOIR. Used by permission of Counterpoint.

"Ten Thousand Flowers" by Wu Men [p. 47, 4l.] from THE ENLIGHTENED HEART: AN ANTHOLOGY OF SACRED POETRY, EDITED by Stephen Mitchell. Copyright © 1989 by Stephen Mitchell. Reprinted by permission of HarperCollins Publishers.

Distributed in Canada by Raincoast Books

Copyright © 2014 by Christopher Willard
    Instant Help Books
    An Imprint of New Harbinger Publications, Inc.
    5674 Shattuck Avenue
    Oakland, CA 94609
    www.newharbinger.com

Cover design by Amy Shoup; Edited by Karen Schader; Acquired by Jess O'Brien

Library of Congress Cataloging-in-Publication Data

Willard, Christopher (Psychologist)
  Mindfulness for teen anxiety : a workbook for overcoming anxiety at home, at school, and everywhere else / Christopher Willard, PsyD.
     pages cm
  Summary: "It's hard enough being a teen without having to worry about panic attacks, chronic worry, and feelings of isolation. In Mindfulness for Teen Anxiety, a psychologist offers teen readers proven-effective, mindfulness-based practices to help them cope with their anxiety, identify common triggers (such as dating or school performance), learn valuable time-management skills, and feel calm at home, at school, and with friends"-- Provided by publisher.
  Audience: Age 14-18.
  ISBN 978-1-60882-910-1 (paperback) -- ISBN 978-1-60882-911-8 (pdf e-book) -- ISBN 978-1-60882-912-5 (epub) 1. Anxiety in adolescence--Juvenile literature. 2. Mind and body in adolescence--Juvenile literature. I. Title.
  BF724.3.A57W55 2014
  155.5'1246--dc23
                 2014016269

Printed in the United States of America

16   15   14

10   9   8   7   6   5   4   3   2   1   First printing

Contents

At School

In the Social World

Performing Under Pressure

Bringing It All Together

Introduction

In my years of working with young adults from many different backgrounds and situations, I've found that it is the smartest and most creative ones who suffer the most from anxiety. I believe that anxiety is the result of a smart, creative mind run amok. Think about it—if you are suffering from anxiety, you can probably think of dozens of reasons why your class presentation will go wrong, why the prom will be a disaster, or why your parents will be disappointed in you. The minds of most other people don't generate nearly as many ideas, either positive or anxious.

The good news is that you don't have to be afraid of your own mind any longer. With some help and some hard work, and by using some of the practices in this book, you can get that amazing mind of yours back to working *for* you, not *against* you.

One of the best adages I've heard essentially says that our thoughts can be our greatest servants or our worst masters. This adage rings very true for me as someone who has seen and helped hundreds if not thousands of people overcome anxiety disorders. When our minds are working for us, they can skillfully produce the answer to a math problem, process visual information from dozens of sources while we are driving at sixty miles per hour, or instruct our bodies in the thousands of muscle movements required just to dribble a basketball. But when our brains are misfiring, they can send us the wrong messages—that it's time to panic, that something terrible is about to happen to us or to someone we love—and that's when things start to get really scary in our minds.

It's not entirely clear why some of us have anxiety; researchers still don't completely agree. For a long time, debates raged about nature versus nurture; you've probably even discussed this in your science classes. What we understand today is that anxiety is probably the result of both. You may have genes that make you more vulnerable to anxiety, and you may have experienced situations or stressors that are activating your anxiety.

Whatever the source of your anxiety, this book offers ways to deal with it in the moment, along with practices to help keep it at bay, and discusses some lifestyle changes for reducing stress that may be making your anxiety worse. It includes written exercises and also asks questions, with lines for writing down your responses. Some of these might feel too personal to write in this book, so feel free to write your answers elsewhere, or not at all; if you don't write, at least give the questions some thought.

Many of the tools have been adapted from very ancient practices, and others come from modern psychotherapy techniques. For example, the Body Scan (activity 17) and Lake Meditation (activity 25) are based on mindfulness-based stress reduction, developed by Jon Kabat-Zinn. Thoughts on Parade (activity 20) was adapted from Steven Hayes's acceptance and commitment therapy, and ideas about wise mind (activity 51) are from Marsha Linehan's dialectical behavior therapy. Chris Germer inspired practices like The Compassionate Friend (activity 27), A Pebble for Your Pocket (activity 40), and, with Kristen Neff, Mind and Body (activity 16); the two write about mindful self-compassion. Noah Levine was the source of words to repeat when walking mindfully (activity 30), and Gregory Kramer (with others) developed the concept of insight dialogue (activity 39). My friend Ashley Sitkin helped me with the yoga practice (activity 46), and the acronym RAIN (activity 50) was developed by Michele McDonald.

If you feel like you need motivation, it can help to go through this book with a friend, relative, or therapist. And although you can skip around and just read the parts that feel most important to you, you will get the most out of the book by doing the whole thing start to finish, and regularly practicing what you've learned along the way.

Learning to manage day-to-day anxiety is not going to be an easy path, but it is a path that a lot of other teens and adults have followed successfully, and so can you.

About Anxiety

Some people have a genetic predisposition to anxiety; because of the genes they inherited, they are more likely to develop anxiety disorders than other people. But all of us experience anxiety at some point in our lives, and with good reason. We need a protective alarm system to alert us to danger and help us stay safe.

Having anxiety is like having an oversensitive alarm system that goes off at all the wrong times, keeping us from getting anything done. It can be downright embarrassing in the wrong situation. Or worse, it can end up putting us in more danger because we are so focused on the false alarm that we miss the signals of real danger.

It can be helpful to know what causes your anxiety, but sometimes it feels more important just to know what to do about it. That is the main goal of this book: to give you practical tools you can use for the toughest anxiety-provoking situations. It may feel hard to be young and facing anxiety, but the positive side is that once you work through your anxiety, which you can, you will be able to help yourself and others for the rest of your life.

And there is a lot of good news. For one thing, you are not alone. One in six teens has an anxiety disorder, which means there's a good chance someone else in your group of friends, a few other kids in every classroom you walk into or sports team you play on, and maybe even a few hundred kids in your entire school all have anxiety. In addition, one in four people will develop an anxiety problem in the course of their lives. You could consider yourself lucky to be getting a head start on learning to cope when you are young. But the best news of all is that anxiety gets better. It *is* possible to learn to minimize your anxiety so it comes less often, and to deal with it when it does come, so that it no longer has so much power over you or what you want to do with your life.

1 why do you get anxious?

Like many illnesses, anxiety disorders tend to run in families. You might want to check with your parents and other relatives to see if they have struggled with anxiety and what they have done to overcome it.

Do you know anyone in your family who has or might have anxiety? Maybe a relative who seems high-strung or easily stressed out? If you can, talk to that person and write here what he or she has done to deal with anxiety.

_____

_____

Anxious people often start with this genetic predisposition. From there, certain events in their lives can make them a bit more anxious. If we've had bad experiences with public speaking in the past, it makes sense that we will start to feel anxious just thinking about it in the future. Even just watching someone else struggle with situations like that can teach us to be cautious, but it might also teach us to be anxious, depending on the circumstances. Some of us can get over these events quickly and move on, but for those of us who were born more sensitive, our alarm systems can reset themselves to go off more easily and get in our way even long after we are safe again. And of course, some experiences are far worse than bungling a class presentation and can affect us even more deeply.

What memories stand out for you or make you anxious just to think about?

_____

_____

Does anything you are anxious about stem from a bad experience someone you know has had? If so, write about what happened.

_____

_____

Think of people in your life you can speak with about some of these experiences. Consider friends, relatives, or other trustworthy adults. Write down their names here.

_____

_____

Think about how much of your anxiety you feel comfortable sharing with those people; it doesn't have to be your life story or your worst panic attack. Decide to share a bit with one person in the next week, and notice how you feel before, during, and after sharing.

There are a number of other factors that contribute to developing anxiety. For one thing, we live in a dangerous world. We get so many messages from the media, school, our parents, and our friends regarding what we should worry about, from terrorism to STDs, that it's no wonder we walk around with our alarm systems set to high alert. We each need a reliable alarm system for a dangerous world, but that system should also differentiate between realistic worries and unrealistic ones. This book can help you not believe everything you think or every signal your body sends your way.

What are some messages you've received that tell you the world is a dangerous place?

_____

_____

activity 1 ✳ why do you get anxious?

What are some of your parents' and your friends' biggest worries?

_____

_____

Which, if any, of these worries have you "caught" from them?

_____

_____

So why do you get anxious? It is most likely a combination of your genes, events in your life, and the kind of world you've grown up in. The scientific term for this is the biopsychosocial model, a fancy phrase you can now casually drop into conversation in your next psychology class!

anxiety's aliases 2

Many people, when they first start experiencing anxiety, don't recognize the symptoms. That's because we don't always have experience with anxiety and are not well informed about it. It can be helpful to know what other feelings are often associated with anxiety.

Exercise: Identifying Anxiety by Other Names

Look over this list, and circle any words that you feel most apply to you. Use the blank lines to add other words or phrases about anxiety.

Afraid	Frozen	Terrified
Agitated	Hesitant	Thoughts racing
Alarmed	Jittery	Troubled
Apprehensive	Nervous	Tweaking out
Concerned	Overwhelmed	Uneasy
Edgy	Panicked	Worried
Fearful	Petrified	_____
Freaking out	Restless	_____
Fretful	Scared	_____
Frightened	Stressed	

3

recognizing anxiety in your body

We often experience anxiety first in our bodies, and then in our minds. Since physical signs can be an early warning signal that anxiety is coming, getting to know your body, and what it may be trying to tell you, is a helpful first step.

Exercise: Physical Signs

Take a look at this list, and see if any of these are symptoms or signals you get when you are anxious, or just before you get anxious. You can use the blank lines to add any others.

Aching jaw	Headache
Backache	Heartburn or indigestion
Breathing faster and more constricted	Heat in chest
Butterflies in stomach	Light-headedness or dizziness
Chest pains	Muscle tension
Clenching or grinding teeth	Nausea
Cramps	Neck ache
Difficulty sleeping	Pounding heart
Dry mouth	Quavering voice
Feeling numb or tingly	Shaky hands
Feeling unusually hot or cold	Stomachache
Feeling weak	Sweating
Flushed or hot cheeks	Tightness or soreness in throat
Getting colds or flus more often	_____
Goosebumps	_____

your anxiety triggers 4

There are a number of common situations that cause anxiety in even the mellowest of people. You will almost certainly face many of these situations at some point in your life, if you haven't faced them already.

Anxiety is often hardest to manage when it comes on unexpectedly, so knowing in advance what situations are likely to trigger your anxiety is half the work of managing it. The more you know yourself, the better off you will be in terms of knowing what skills will work in those situations.

Exercise: Common Anxiety Triggers

On a scale from 0 to 5 (with 5 being most anxious), rate how anxious each of these common triggers makes you feel, and then consider how much of a priority dealing with that situation is. For example, public speaking might make you really anxious, but if you don't have to do it often, it could be a low priority.

Over time, you can definitely lower your anxiety about any of these triggers, especially by using the practices in this book. You might not be able to get all of them to zero, but you can probably lower most of them.

_____ Being alone

_____ Being bored

_____ Dating

_____ Driving

_____ Going to school

_____ Grades

_____ Health concerns

_____ Insomnia

_____ Interviews

_____ Living in a chaotic house

_____ Monday mornings

_____ One-on-one interactions

_____ Parties and social events

_____ Performing in public

_____ Phobias*

_____ Public speaking

_____ Social situations

_____ Stress at home

_____ Studying

_____ Sunday evenings

_____ Talking to teachers

_____ Tests and exams

_____ Trying to sleep

_____ Writer's block

_____ Your family

* Phobias are fears that can cause anxiety. Some people are phobic about snakes, which is not much of a problem unless you live in a jungle or work at a zoo. But others are phobic about germs or social situations, which can be pretty hard to avoid without major disruption to your life. Some common phobias that can get in your way include traveling, being in small spaces, and visiting doctors' offices, among others.

tracking your anxiety 5

Looking at your patterns of anxiety over the course of an average day and week can help you respond proactively, rather than react with panic in the moment. You don't have to keep a journal about every second of every day, but it might be helpful to fill out this chart and look for patterns so you can anticipate challenges.

Exercise: Anxiety Record

Before completing this chart, make copies for later use. At the end of each day, write down situations that made you anxious at different times. Record the kinds of thoughts and physical sensations you were having for each situation, then rate your anxiety on a scale from 1 to 5, with 5 being most anxious.

Day _____				
	Morning	Afternoon	Evening	Nighttime
Situation				
Thoughts				
Physical Sensations				
Anxiety Rating				

At the start of each week, look over your charts for the week before to help you anticipate upcoming situations that may cause anxiety.

6 avoidance and distraction traps

Anxiety is uncomfortable in our minds as well as in our bodies. The natural thing to do when we feel uncomfortable is to try to lessen the discomfort or make it end as quickly as possible. We might also avoid situations that make us uncomfortable in the first place.

These strategies can help in the short run but backfire in the long run. You can never live life to its fullest if you avoid *everything* that makes you uncomfortable. If you kept on avoiding, you would never ask out that boy or girl on a date; if you never participate in class, you might end up with a bad grade. Plus, when you avoid too often, you tend to start avoiding a lot of things, and friends and family may wonder what is going on, increasing your shame and creating a whole cycle of avoidance.

As if that weren't enough, avoidance can often make anxiety worse. As you start to avoid things that make you anxious, you get a bit of short-term relief, so you avoid more and more. At the same time, you miss out on the chance to learn that the thing you feared probably wouldn't have been that bad after all. Avoidance becomes a habit, and the thing you are avoiding only gets bigger in your mind.

Exercise: Coping Activities

There are both healthy and unhealthy ways of coping with anxiety, and you've probably already discovered a few yourself. Do you recognize any of the following in yourself or people around you who are also anxious? Circle the ones you find yourself doing, and think about whether you could trade some of the less healthy ones for healthier ones.

Healthy	Unhealthy	Okay in Moderation
Community service	Avoiding people	Buying yourself something nice
Dancing	Avoiding situations	Computer/tablet time
Drawing or painting	Bingeing on sweets	Food
Eating a healthy meal	Blaming others	Personal grooming
Exercising	Cutting or self-harm	Sleeping
Listening to music	Drinking	Social media
Looking at artwork	Drugs	TV or movies
Playing music	Isolating yourself from friends	Video games
Reading	Skipping class	
Spending time with friends or family		
Studying		
Taking care of your pet		
Writing		

Healthy distractions can be helpful ways to cope with anxiety, but it is important that they not veer into avoidance of other responsibilities in your life.

7 keeping your body healthy

Yes, your grandmother was right! Taking care of your body is important not only to your physical health but also to your mental health. Here are a few quick tips for basic body maintenance that can help keep your anxiety at bay, or at levels you can manage.

Getting Enough Sleep

Your body absolutely needs sleep to have the energy to keep anxiety at bay, but I know what a lot of young people say when I bring this up: "Yeah right. With SATs this Saturday, the big dance on Saturday night, and an English essay due on Monday?"

Maybe getting a lot of sleep isn't as easy as you would like it to be, but it will make a big difference. Just as important as getting enough sleep, though, is getting quality sleep. Even just going to bed and waking up around the same time daily—staying within a "sleep window"—can make a big difference in how well you sleep and how well you function. And if that means not sleeping in so much on the weekends, give it a shot for a couple of weeks and see if it helps how you feel.

How much sleep are you getting on the average weeknight?

_____

How much sleep are you getting on the average weekend?

_____

Do you go to bed and wake up around the same time?

_____

What is your bedtime routine? Is it relaxing to your mind and body, like washing and reading, or is it stimulating, like eating and screen time?

_____

_____

_____

Getting Enough Exercise

Maybe you're already a high school athlete, so getting exercise isn't an issue. But even if you are an athlete, it might help to cross-train with exercise that doesn't have the stress of competition or performance associated with it. Consider dance, yoga, martial arts, or another practice. Find something that allows you to move your body without worries about how well you are performing for teammates, coaches, and spectators.

If you find it hard to motivate yourself, make an exercise playlist, or find a podcast, an audiobook, or some comedy to listen to while you work out. You'll feel better in the moment, and exercise will also help you concentrate more effectively and think more creatively. It will boost your mood and lower your overall anxiety. In fact, a little jog up and down the stairs during a break on the SATs or before a stressful speech can really lower your anxiety and improve your performance. Skeptical? Try it once or twice. An added plus is that getting exercise will help you sleep.

What days and times can you set aside to get some exercise? Take out your calendar and mark them down.

_____

_____

What are some ways you can exercise if you don't exercise already? For example, could you walk to school, take the stairs instead of the elevator, jog, or take a yoga class?

_____

_____

What are some of your favorite forms of exercise you can do alone? With friends?

_____

_____

How are your anxiety and stress levels after you've exercised compared to before?

_____

_____

Eating Healthy

Breakfast is essential, even if you don't like to eat in the morning or your anxiety makes your stomach too nervous. Start with something easy to digest—trail mix, bananas, yogurt, or dry toast—and see if you can work up from there. Cut down on sugar, and eat more small meals if you have to, but remember that your body and mind need to have enough energy to keep going.

Are you eating three meals a day? How healthy are they?

_____

_____

What are some foods you are able to eat even with a nervous stomach?

_____

_____

What are some of your favorite healthy foods?

_____

_____

Cutting Down on Alcohol and Drugs

Alcohol and drugs (and that definitely includes caffeine) may seem to help you relax in the short run, but the medium- and long-term effects can wreak havoc on your body and mind, leaving you vulnerable to anxiety. If you are hungover, your body and mind will be even more vulnerable to anxiety creeping back. Caffeine in coffee, tea, and energy drinks might keep you going while you're studying but will seriously raise your anxiety level. Think about it—many physical symptoms of anxiety are pretty much the same as the physical symptoms of drinking too much caffeine.

What's your substance intake like these days?

_____

_____

Can you cut down for a few weeks and see if it makes a difference in your overall anxiety?

_____

_____

Relaxing

Last, and most important, *relax*. When you can relax your mind and your body, a visit from anxiety will be far less likely. We all have different ways to relax. Here are a few suggestions: take a bath or shower, practice yoga, take a walk, do some crafting, or try some of the healthy distractions listed in exercise 6.

What are some ways you like to relax?

_____

_____

Which of these can you fit into your schedule?

_____

_____

The acronym HALT is one quick way to remember some of these self-care tips. Check in a few times a day and ask yourself: *Am I hungry? Am I angry? Am I lonely? Am I tired?* If you answer yes to any of those, think of a healthy way you can respond to those needs.

finding balance 8

Living a balanced life is one of the biggest challenges we face, and everything gets worse when we are stressed. I've heard it said that the average student needs time for three things—sleep, social life, and studying—but has time for only two. Does that feel accurate to you? If you focus on schoolwork and sleep, there's no time for a social life; if you focus on school and socializing, there's no way you're sleeping enough; and if you spend your time focusing on friendships and sleep, you're probably failing your classes. And what about sports, family, jobs, and the countless other concerns young people face, stressing themselves out by feeling as if there is always something more they could be doing? When your time is at a premium, your stress goes up, raising the likelihood of your anxiety getting worse.

Of sleep, social life, and studying, which do you find yourself emphasizing, and which do you find yourself neglecting or sacrificing?

_____

_____

_____

_____

9 don't believe everything you think!

Let's say you and a good friend have agreed to meet at the movie theater at 7:15. It's now 7:30, and you're waiting outside the theater, but your friend hasn't arrived yet and hasn't texted or called. Many people would just think, *My friend is probably running late and will be here any minute.* But for anxious people, it can go in any number of ways. Some may think the worst: *There's been a terrible accident; my friend may be hurt!* Others take it personally: *My friend probably forgot about me because I'm not that important to him.* Or maybe even *She ditched me to hang out with someone else. She probably doesn't even want to be my friend anymore.* Others might blame themselves: *I must have gotten the time wrong. I'm so stupid!*

The anxious mind can get quite creative, can't it? Next time you find yourself in a situation like this, see if you can invent wilder stories on purpose, rather than having your anxiety take over and tell you the stories.

Exercise: Telling Your Own Stories

Imagine that your parents tell you they both will be gone for a week, and you will be alone in the house. What might happen to your parents? What might happen to you when you're alone? List all the possible bad situations and worst-case scenarios you can think of.

_____

_____

_____

_____

_____

Look back over your list. Circle the things you can control, and underline those you can't.

Knowing that you cannot control or change certain situations, what can you do? Perhaps you've heard these words:

> *Grant me the serenity*
> *to accept the things I cannot change,*
> *the courage to change the things I can,*
> *and the wisdom to know the difference.*

Whether you are a person of faith or not, it can be helpful to list your worries, then mark your list to show what you can and cannot change. This approach can be almost like a formula you apply to any difficult situation, helping you determine a clear plan of action in a cloud of worry and emotion.

Write down a situation that makes you anxious.

_____

_____

What can you do to change this situation for the better?

_____

_____

What do you not have the power to change about this situation?

_____

_____

What could help you let go of worrying about it so much?

_____

_____

Exercise: Recognizing Thoughts as Thoughts

So, what if you could remind yourself that all these stories you're telling yourself are just thoughts, not necessarily reality? It is far easier said than done, of course, but you could start by putting the words *I'm having the thought that...* in front of every anxious thought you have. For example, instead of thinking *I'm going to fail the test*, tell yourself, *I'm having the thought that I'm going to fail the test*.

Write down three anxious thoughts here, then rewrite them, adding the words "I'm having the thought that..."

_____

_____

_____

_____

_____

_____

anxiety in disguise 10

Sometimes our strong emotions get clouded and confused with each other. Strong emotions can also cause us to act out in self-destructive ways. That's why mindfulness, introduced in the next section, can be so helpful. It allows us to see our true emotions more clearly and to respond to them in healthy ways.

Anxiety and Anger

When Tim was younger, he would lie in bed listening to his parents argue into the night and would worry about what was going to happen. *Would they split up? Were they angry with him?* As he got older, he tried to intervene in their arguments and would end up caught in the middle, with everyone in the family angry with everyone else.

Tim began to associate anxiety with anger, which started to get in the way of his schoolwork. Even his friends became wary of him. When he got on the basketball court, his aggression often led to fouls, which hurt his whole team. Tim's coach taught him a few basic breathing practices to help him keep his cool during games. Soon Tim was able to see more clearly that underneath his anger and aggression was simple anxiety. He started working on that anxiety, and not only did his anxiety and anger improve, but so did his team's performance.

Have you ever noticed that some other emotion, like anger or irritability, comes over you when you feel anxious? List a few of those emotions here.

_____

_____

_____

Anxiety and Sadness

Emily's brother had leukemia when they were both young, and Emily was often scared of what might happen to him. Her family was scared too, but they had a hard time knowing how to talk about it. Emily ended up learning that it was better to be quiet than to talk about her anxiety, and so when she was anxious she would keep to herself and feel sad.

Over time, sadness and numbness started to take the place of anxiety, and rather than get anxious when things got overwhelming, she would become depressed instead. Emily asked her parents if she could talk to a therapist to help her deal with the depression. She and her therapist began to see a pattern: whenever she was stressed or anxious, her depression would emerge. When she learned to manage her anxiety, she no longer became so depressed. With some hard work and a skillful therapist, she managed to interrupt the cycle between her anxiety and depression. Soon both began to improve, and her life became fuller and happier.

Are there times when you felt your anxiety was buried under a layer of depression or sadness? List a few of those here.

_____

_____

_____

Anxiety and Acting Out

Tina had a long list of coping mechanisms that included scratching herself until she bled, smoking cigarettes, doing drugs, and other behaviors that her parents and friends worried about. She never realized that these unhealthy behaviors were essentially a way of covering up her anxiety, and neither did anyone else.

In a mindfulness group, she learned to start paying attention to her feelings and what triggered her urges to act out in unhealthy ways. She realized that underneath these urges and behaviors was anxiety. First she would feel anxious, and the next thing she knew she was scratching herself or lighting up another cigarette. Practicing mindfulness and other techniques allowed her to watch her thoughts and urges, and see the anxiety come but also go. She learned to ride out all the urges to shut off her feelings of anxiety with dangerous and self-destructive behaviors.

Are there times when you've acted out in destructive or self-destructive ways because you were anxious, or do you know people who have done so? Write about some of those times here.

_____

_____

_____

For other people, anxiety manifests as altogether different behaviors or emotions, or even a mix of emotions.

When, and in what disguises, have you seen your anxiety?

_____

_____

How did you recognize it underneath?

_____

_____

11 building on your strengths

There is a lot more to you than just your anxiety. Positive psychology is the idea that our strengths are just as important, if not more important, to recognize and understand as our weaknesses. Our strengths are what we rely on to get us through hard situations. In addition to our inner strengths, we may also have people who support us.

Exercise: All About You

Imagine for a moment that you are being interviewed by a reporter who is writing an article about you for your adoring fans. For each question, write down the first thing that comes to mind.

What are your greatest talents?

_____

_____

What are your biggest strengths?

_____

_____

What do your friends admire and like about you?

_____

_____

What are some of the hardest things you've been through in your life, and how did you get through them?

_____

_____

What advice would you give to a friend who is anxious, stressed, or having a hard time?

_____

_____

Who is your favorite role model for overcoming hard times, and why?

_____

_____

Do you have a favorite inspirational quote, poem, or song that helps you through hard times? What is its message?

_____

_____

What important events and people made you the person you are today?

_____

_____

Which people are there for you when you need them? (This may include friends, relatives, teachers, mental-health professionals, coworkers, classmates, teammates, coaches, siblings, and clergy, among others.)

_____

_____

12 thought distortions

The more anxious we are, and the longer we are anxious, the more likely we are to be thinking in patterns that are distorted and no longer reflect the reality of our situations. Here are a few of the most common ways that anxious people tend to see the world.

Black-and-White Thinking

Black-and-white thinking is an all-or-nothing approach—deciding that things must be all bad or all good rather than seeing them as complicated.

> *Becca was shy. She had agreed to go to the winter dance with a large group of friends, even though she wasn't so crazy about the idea. Dinner beforehand with friends was fun, and so was the ride over. But as soon as she got to the dance, she started to feel anxious about all the kids she didn't know so well. Rather than remembering that there would be some stressful or awkward moments and some fun ones at the dance, she decided that she hated the whole thing and just about everyone there, and she spent the evening clinging to one friend before leaving early.*

Have you ever been tripped up by black-and-white thinking, when in fact the situation was more complicated? Describe what happened.

_____

_____

Discounting the Positive

This thought distortion involves looking only at the negative and failing to see the positive. The result is a pessimistic, anxious view of the world.

> *After Anthony scored the winning goal in his soccer game, the coach made him a starter on the varsity team, rather than second string. But before long, Anthony started*

psyching himself out, feeling like a fraud and thinking the only reason he'd scored was because the other team's goalie had made a mistake. He had been practicing for weeks and was one of the fastest players on the team, but rather than seeing what he had done to contribute to his own success, he decided that his success was due only to accidents. He got so anxious as a varsity starter that his anxiety interfered with his game and he ended up back as a benchwarmer.

Have there been times when you discounted the positive and only looked at the negative reasons why something good happened? Describe what happened.

_____

_____

Catastrophizing

Catastrophizing means seeing everything as a disaster, or making big assumptions based on minimal evidence.

Jessica had a stomachache for three days in a row and started to worry about it. Pretty soon she was completely freaking out, unable to sleep and absolutely convinced that she had some kind of allergy, or maybe even stomach cancer. Or could she be pregnant? The more she read about it online, the worse she felt, and the gloomier her thoughts became. By the time she saw a doctor, she was convinced she had only a few months to live. But it turned out she had irritable bowel syndrome, a common health issue for people with anxiety. Soon she was treating her anxiety, and her stomachaches faded.

Have you ever catastrophized a situation? Describe what happened.

_____

_____

Emotional Reasoning

In the heat of the moment, when we are particularly emotional, it can be very hard to think clearly and rationally. Something feels real or like it's true, and so we believe that it must be real or true.

> *Ashley always felt exhausted after taking a test, partly because she had so much nervous energy. She left almost every exam feeling terrible, which she assumed meant she must have failed, and yet her grades were usually good. When she talked to her parents about it, she began to realize that feeling terrible after a test did not mean that her performance actually was terrible.*

Have you ever used emotional reasoning, listening to your feelings too much, rather than your thoughts? Describe what happened.

Perfectionism

Many anxious people suffer from perfectionism; they feel as though anything they can't do perfectly is not worth doing at all.

> *Taylor felt like she had to be the best athlete, best student, and most popular and talented girl in school, or it wasn't even worth trying. Because she set her expectations so high, there was no way she could possibly hope to meet them. This left her forever disappointed in herself, and anxious about everything. She and I worked together to set realistic, internal, and personal goals for success, rather than measuring herself against others all the time. She found it helpful to remember that all she ever knew about how perfect anyone else was was what they showed the world.*

Have you ever been a bit of a perfectionist? Describe what happened.

Exercise: Words to Watch Out For

Many of the following words are associated with thought distortions. Over the next few days, pay attention to how often you find yourself saying these dangerous words, whether out loud or in your mind.

All	Everyone	Must	None
Always	Everything	Never	Should
Every	Have to	No one	

When do you find yourself saying these words?

_____

_____

How do they make you feel when you say them?

_____

_____

How true are they?

_____

_____

13 worrying on purpose

Once our thoughts are under way, it can be really hard to turn them off. Just try this: don't think about a pink elephant for the next minute. And...go!

Did that work? Probably not. In fact, often the more we try *not* to think about something, the more we end up thinking about it. The fact is, when you are anxious, the parts of your brain that think rationally almost completely shut down, making it nearly impossible to reason with yourself. At times like that, you need to sidestep rational thought and try something completely different. As Albert Einstein said, "No problem can be solved from the same level of consciousness that created it," and he was a pretty smart guy.

Here's the positive: the more we try to think about something, the harder it can be.

Try thinking about your biggest worry right now. What is it?

_____

_____

Now set a timer and give yourself a full two minutes to do nothing but worry. What happened?

_____

_____

After a few minutes of deliberately worrying, many people find that their minds actually get tired of worrying and move on to something else. Eventually, that will happen for your mind as well. It can be helpful to set aside five or ten minutes once or twice a day to worry on purpose; you can put a reminder in your phone or on your calendar and try it for yourself. Better for you to find your anxiety and face it than to wait around for it to find you!

Writing down your anxious thoughts is another way to get them out of your head, and research shows that writing down worries and then tearing them up and throwing them away can actually help.

Summing Up

In this section, you hopefully learned a bit about what anxiety is and where it comes from. You also got a better sense of what makes you anxious and the times and triggers that heighten your anxiety. Anxiety can be like other unpleasant things we encounter: we want to get rid of it, avoid it, or find a way to experience it less intensely. Unfortunately, there are times when these strategies don't work, or even make things worse. You learned that anxiety is very common—and very manageable. You learned about ways to identify anxiety, especially when it disguises itself, and practiced a few healthy coping strategies. Now that you know your anxiety a little better, you can be less afraid of it.

Take a moment now to reflect on the lessons, skills, and practices in this section.

What activity did you relate to most?

_____

_____

Which skills do you think you would be most likely to use in your daily life?

_____

_____

Which skills do you think you can try in the next week?

_____

_____

Mindfulness: Paying Attention to the Present

There is an old story about a traveler who met a meditation guru at a remote mountaintop temple. The traveler asked, "What is it you do here that is so special? It seems to me that all you do is work and eat and walk around all day. That's just what we do back in the city." The master paused for a moment before responding, "But when we work, we know we are working; when we eat, we know we are eating; and when we walk, we know we are walking."

That is what mindfulness is all about: doing one thing and being fully aware of what you are doing. You might want to think about it in terms that make sense to you; for example, *When I'm studying, I know I'm studying; when I'm running, I know I'm running; when I'm shooting hoops, I know I'm shooting hoops.*

Mindfulness is paying attention to what is happening in the present moment, noticing when and where your mind may wander and bringing it back. It may sound hard, because our minds have a tendency to wander, but mindfulness, like any other skill, is something we can develop with practice.

14 what does mindfulness have to do with anxiety?

Anxiety sneaks up when we are paying attention to everything *but* the present moment. Anxiety comes when we are too focused on the future, the what-if scenarios we have no control over.

Say you have a big test coming up. If you're anxious, you'll probably start imagining that you'll fail the test. Spinning out from there, you might imagine that you'll never get into college, end up jobless, and die homeless, alone and unloved—a detailed tragedy that ends years in the future. There you are, envisioning your miserable end instead of just planning for tomorrow's test!

By staying in the moment, which is the essence of mindfulness, we keep that story from getting away from us; we just focus on what is right in front of us and give it our full attention.

If you try any of the practices in this book for very long, you'll notice that your thoughts begin to wander. That does not mean you're doing anything wrong; your mind is just doing what it does: creating thoughts and thinking them. As a teacher of mine once said, "The mind creates thoughts like the heart pumps blood and the mouth secretes saliva." We cannot and probably should not try to shut them off altogether. The trick of mindfulness is to be aware that you are thinking.

One question many anxious people ask is, *Why would I want to pay attention to my thoughts? My thoughts are the very problem I'm trying to get away from!* It's a good point. But I think—in fact I *know*—that if you pay attention to your overwhelming thoughts, they can start to seem a lot less overwhelming. In mindfulness practice, we see all our thoughts and feelings and urges as they really are, without distracting ourselves. We can then choose which ones we want to pay attention to, which ones we want to believe and respond to from a place of wisdom and calm.

Here is an example of how truly paying attention can be helpful, and how not paying attention can get us anxious and worked up.

Amelia was out on a date with Jake. They saw a movie, then took a long walk. The date was going so well that neither of them wanted it to end, so they went for ice cream.

Amelia took the first few bites of her ice cream. Her taste buds were telling her Give me more of that! *She could also feel messages from her stomach:* I dunno, I'm kinda full here. *Meanwhile, her mom's suggestion to just relax and enjoy herself was in the mix, but so was a friend's advice: "Don't eat a lot in front of boys or they'll think you're a pig." Not knowing which voice to listen to, she began to panic, wondering what to do or say as she felt her chest tightening and her heart racing. She mumbled something to Jake about not feeling well and rushed out, feeling like a total loser. The next day was worse, as she started to worry about what Jake might say to everyone else back at school.*

But imagine if Amelia had brought some mindfulness to the situation. Aware of all those voices, she could have listened to the wisest of them. She could have slowed down, paid attention, and calmly decided what she wanted to do before the anxiety took over and she took off. Instead, she ended up getting hijacked by anxiety, and slunk home feeling embarrassed.

Describe a situation when you were overwhelmed by too many thoughts rather than being able to pay attention to just one at a time.

_____

_____

What are some situations where a bit of mindfulness could have helped you?

_____

_____

The practice of mindfulness gives us insight into the ways our own minds function. Each time we manage to stay in the present moment for a little longer, each time we remember and anticipate our thought patterns and forgive our brains for making thoughts, the right solution to whatever problem we are facing at the moment is that much more likely to arise naturally and calmly.

15 the power of singletasking

Another way to describe mindfulness is to think of it as singletasking—just doing what you are doing, aware of what you are doing, without doing anything else. This is not how we typically operate in our modern multitasking world, so it can feel a bit unfamiliar. But it can also feel good, relaxing and centering us.

Multitasking can also feel good because we feel as though we're getting a lot of small things done, but research shows that we are actually less efficient when we multitask than when we do just one thing at a time. Worse, when we multitask, life seems more chaotic, which only increases our anxiety. So before you write off this idea of singletasking, try this practice for less than a minute.

Mindfulness Practice: Singletasking

- Close your eyes, and place one finger lightly on your forehead.

- Take a breath, and just notice what this sensation feels like.

- Notice what your finger feels like against your forehead. Notice what your forehead feels like against your finger. Become aware of texture, temperature, maybe even your pulse, and any other aspects of sensation from this simple action of awareness in this very moment.

- Take another ten seconds to just notice and allow for any sensations and thoughts.

How do you feel after trying this practice?

_____

_____

Was it helpful? If so, in what situations could you see yourself using it?

_____

_____

bodily tension 16

Having a sense of what mindfulness feels like in your body can help you identify when you are being mindful and when you are not. With that awareness, you can move from tension to a more mindful frame of mind.

Mindfulness Practice: Mind and Body

- First, sit up rigidly straight, tensing your back muscles and flexing your shoulders. Hold your hands out in front of you in fists. Notice what this feels like in your body. How does it feel to breathe in this position? What emotions come? What kinds of thoughts arise? Can you think of recent times when your body felt like this?

- Next, allow your body to slump over, with your back slouching, all your muscles released, and your head falling down. Notice what this new position feels like in your body. How does it feel to breathe in this position? What emotions come? What kinds of thoughts arise? When have you felt like this recently?

- Now sit up straight. Hold your hands out, but not too tensely, perhaps resting on your knees, and with your palms open and upward. Your head and chest should be lifted, but not tense. Notice how this shift feels in your body. How does it feel to breathe in this position? What emotions come? What kinds of thoughts arise? Are there times when you feel like this?

These few positions show how different mind states feel in our bodies. In the first position, making fists, most people report feeling tense, stressed, angry, ready to fight, or even just anxious. They feel closed off to new ideas, with not many thoughts. This is the physical state of the fight-or-flight response, and it is what happens when we try to resist what is going on in our world and end up stressed by it. Check in with your body throughout the day and week, and as you do, you might want to notice whether you are carrying any tension like this, physically or emotionally, and to just let it go.

The second posture, slumped over, although relaxing, is perhaps a bit too relaxed and passive. A lot of people feel sleepy or overwhelmed or just feel like giving up in this position. We want to be aware of times when we are feeling this way, and find ways to reenergize ourselves. Sometimes people ask, "If relaxation is important, why shouldn't I just sit around and watch TV when I'm stressed?" The answer is that you end up in this passive state of overrelaxation that comes close to feeling helpless and like giving up, rather than in an alert state of openness, like the next posture brings.

This third position represents mindfulness, openness, and active acceptance, rather than passive acceptance or active resistance. We are as awake and alert as possible without inviting tension, and as relaxed as possible without giving up. We are at the proper balance in our bodies and minds. This is the mental and physical posture we want to aim for in most of life's situations, in order to be open and able to respond to whatever comes our way.

Often, when we start to feel anxious or approach a triggering situation, shifting our pose into one of mindfulness, even for just a few seconds, can make a tremendous difference in how we feel. Our minds and bodies are much more connected than we often give them credit for being.

body scan 17

As you read earlier, much of our anxiety begins in the body, overflows to the mind, and then just hijacks the whole mind-body system. But when we really start paying attention to the body, we can sense anxiety at the moment it begins and head it off before it snowballs, reaches our minds, and leaves us totally overwhelmed. The more we know our bodies, the more likely we are to be able to stop that snowball before it becomes an avalanche.

So how do we get to know our bodies? By now you've probably caught on and are thinking *through mindfulness*. And that's right! Follow the script below, and you'll pretty quickly get a sense of what to do. You can also record yourself reading the script, or do this with a friend, family member, or therapist reading along. With practice, your mind will get in the habit of automatically checking in with your body, even just for a moment, without needing a reminder. It's the same way that practice helps you automatically do a multiplication table or perform on the soccer field.

For some people, getting in touch with the body might be harder than for others. Maybe you feel as though your body has betrayed you in the past through sickness, or through weight gain or loss; maybe you don't like your body; or maybe thinking about certain parts of your body can bring up some bad memories or emotions. If any of these is the case for you, I'd encourage you to be extra cautious with this practice, and consider doing it with someone you trust.

Mindfulness Practice: Body Scan Script

- Find a comfortable place, preferably one where you can lie down on your back undisturbed for about five or ten minutes. Close your eyes. Allow whatever surface you are on to just hold you, and trust your body to breathe for you.

- Start by simply bringing your awareness to your breath. As you breathe in, allow your awareness to flow into and throughout your body, and notice the body's various points of contact with the surface beneath you.

- Once again, bring your awareness to your breath, following it down your throat and past your belly and imagining it reaching all the way down into your legs and feet. As you bring your awareness into your toes, just notice any sensations there. Notice temperature, moisture, the sensation of socks if you're wearing them, your skin…and then deeper under the surface, feeling the muscles and bones deep under the skin.

- Follow your breath once more into your feet, aware of any other sensations in this part of your body. Take a moment just to be with them and notice how they feel. Your feet have been carrying you around all day. You may want to send them some gratitude for their hard work. As you breathe in again, follow your awareness into your ankles and calves. Breathe again now into your knees and thighs, exploring any sensations there.

- Now follow the breath into your lower back, aware that the lower back can be a place where we store tension and anxiety.

- On the next breath, follow your awareness around to your abdomen. Feel the movement as your belly rises and falls.

- Next, breathe into the upper back and shoulders, another place where stress can hide.

- Let go now of your back and shoulders, and bring your awareness into your chest, exploring this area and what it might be telling you.

- Next, gently follow the breath into your fingertips and your hands. Breathing in once more, follow your awareness into your wrists, into your forearms, and upward into your upper arms and shoulders, aware of the sensations and your body and mind responding to these sensations.

- Now breathe awareness into the back of your head, being aware of how your head feels, and on the next breath into the crown of your head, into your forehead, and down into your face. Just notice sensations as they arise, and notice thoughts or emotions or urges that go with them, watching them change with each breath.

- Take a moment now to thank the parts of your body for their hard work in keeping you alive and healthy. Then quickly scan through the body once more for any tension or discomfort, and just breathe into that part of the body for a few breaths.

- And now, begin to shift your attention from deep inside your body toward the outside, bringing your awareness into the room around you. Feel the soft surface underneath you, and allow your eyes to gently open, knowing that you can take this new awareness and comfort with your body into the rest of your day and life.

How did you feel in your mind during and after this practice?

_____

_____

In your body?

_____

_____

What feelings and urges came up?

_____

_____

Did sensations stay constant or did they change?

_____

_____

What emotions did you notice in your body?

_____

_____

How did you respond to discomfort, physically and emotionally?

_____

_____

18 bringing mindfulness to your anxiety

Have you ever been so nervous about a game that you forgot your equipment you needed for it? Or so worried about a test that you didn't notice you'd walked past your classroom? Have you ever seen an old cartoon where a character caught up in thought and worry crashes right into a brick wall? These scenarios show that when we are captive to anxiety we are often not paying attention to what is right in front of us. Staying in the present, we have to deal only with the present, not emotions and thoughts about the future.

Try this simple two-minute experiment. Find a spot without distractions, sit down, and do nothing for two minutes: no texting, no music, no TV, no fidgeting. You can set a timer on your phone, or you might even want to try the website http://www .donothingfor2minutes.com. Take these two minutes to just notice what is happening in your mind, in your body, and in the room around you.

What were your thoughts during these two minutes? And right now?

_____

_____

What kinds of emotions and feelings were you having during the time? And right now?

_____

_____

What did you notice in your body during those two minutes, and what can you feel in your body right now?

_____

_____

How did you respond when distractions came up?

_____

_____

One of the most important parts of the practice of mindfulness is not judging ourselves for having thoughts. You don't have to like your thoughts, but try to let go of feeling ashamed of them. My favorite way of thinking about the mind is as a puppy that just wanders around in search of anything interesting, sometimes getting itself into trouble. What's the best way to train a puppy? It's not by making the puppy feel bad, but by gently picking it up and bringing it back to a safer place over and over again, with a patient smile on your face.

We start to learn about our anxiety by bringing mindfulness to it, or to certain triggers. We do this by paying attention to what is happening in our minds and bodies as we start down the path of anxiety.

Once again, sit still for a moment or two (it doesn't have to be a full two minutes this time), and take a few deep breaths to clear your mind. Remember, you don't have to like what you notice; just notice it. Take a moment now to bring your thoughts to the subject of school.

What kinds of emotions did you notice?

_____

_____

What kinds of thoughts came up?

_____

_____

Did you notice any changes in your body or physical sensations?

_____

_____

Now bring your mind to friends and dating.

What kinds of emotions did you notice?

_____

_____

What kinds of thoughts came up?

_____

_____

Did you notice any changes in your body or physical sensations?

_____

_____

Now try bringing your mind to your family: parents, siblings, and other relatives.

What kinds of emotions did you notice?

_____

_____

What kinds of thoughts came up?

_____

_____

Did you notice any changes in your body or physical sensations?

_____

_____

What are some situations that really get your anxiety going? Bring them to mind, and then write about what emotions, thoughts, and physical sensations come up with them.

_____

_____

Pay attention over the next few days and notice where your mind tends to wander. Are there times, places, situations, or people who trigger certain reactions?

19 the present moment

You may have heard wise people talk about the importance of living in the moment, being in the here and now, or staying present. I myself had heard this advice for many years without ever really understanding what it meant. Then one day, it just hit me. *If I'm in the moment, I'm not in the future, worrying about what could possibly happen to me or to people I love. If I'm in the here and now, my mind is not halfway across town, wondering what some other person thinks of me. If I'm in the present, I'm not stuck feeling bad about the past, about things that happened to me or things I did. And in the present, things are actually pretty okay.* Suddenly, the whole idea of staying in the present moment started to make a lot more sense.

Of course, staying in the present moment is easier said than done. Sometimes we have to make plans for the future, and it's always important to examine the past to learn from it. The problem comes when we are too focused on the future, which tends to make us anxious, or too focused on the past, which can tend to get us depressed. I once heard someone say, "Make plans, but don't plan on the outcomes." I think that's pretty good advice about finding the balance of how much to focus on the future. The other reality is that things are usually okay in the present moment; for the most part, bad things exist in the future we imagine or the past we can't let go of. And if bad things *are* happening in the present, they don't usually last that long.

What are some times planning for the future has helped you?

_____

_____

What are some times you have gotten stuck thinking about the future too much?

_____

_____

What are some lessons you have learned from the past?

_____

_____

What are some times you have been stuck in the past or wished you could change it?

_____

_____

What are some times you have been able to be fully in the present moment?

_____

_____

How did those moments feel?

_____

_____

20 visualizing the present

Mindfulness is basically just paying attention to what is actually happening in the present moment. The present moment is usually not so bad because, after all, you're alive and breathing, even if you're uncomfortable or things feel uncertain. So with mindfulness, we watch what is happening in the present moment, sometimes paying attention to things outside us, sometimes to things inside us, but mostly just keeping our mind and attention trained on the present without wandering too far into the past or future.

Let's practice now by imagining our thoughts going by without getting caught up in where they come from, or where they're going, just noticing them as they arrive and then letting them go.

Mindfulness Practice: Thoughts on Parade

- Take a moment to find a comfortable posture, and just begin to bring your awareness to your thoughts.

- Imagine a parade going by on the street; you are sitting or standing and watching the parade go past.

- Now try to imagine each of your thoughts actually on the floats going past, or perhaps on signs and banners carried by marchers in the parade. Take a few minutes, and just imagine the thoughts passing by.

- Remember, don't join the parade and start marching with the thoughts; just stand back and enjoy the show, knowing that even the biggest thoughts will pass by or be carried away by someone in the parade.

What did you notice during this practice?

_____

_____

How do you feel after this practice?

_____

_____

There are all kinds of ways we can imagine our thoughts passing other than in a parade. Try a few of these and see which one fits you best.

- Boats or other objects float past on a beautiful river, while you watch from the banks and are careful not to get swept up in the flowing water yourself.

- Cars and traffic rush past on the highway while you stand on an overpass and simply observe them coming and going. The biggest thoughts are in buses or trucks, the smallest in small cars or motorcycles.

- A conveyor belt moves along in a factory, where your job is to inspect each thought as it passes, keeping the good ones moving and tossing out the mistakes.

- Thoughts float by in bubbles.

- Thoughts drift past on clouds in the sky.

- Follow the bouncing ball as if you were singing along with a karaoke machine.

- Watch thoughts as scenery passing by on a train.

- See thoughts as fish swimming in a lake that is still and reflective on the surface.

- Stand in the shallow end of the pool, looking at the deep end without slipping. See thoughts in and under the water.

- Sights and sounds arrive at a factory as raw materials; thoughts come out.

activity 20 ✳ visualizing the present

If there is another image that works for you, describe it here, or draw it on a separate piece of paper.

_____

_____

_____

_____

_____

_____

clearing the mind 21

When we are overstressed and overbooked like so many people these days, it becomes hard to see which thoughts and signals are important and worth paying attention to, and which ones are false alarms. The more we have going on, the harder it is to separate our anxious thoughts from our important ones, with the result that we become overwhelmed.

It can help to imagine that your mind is a snow globe, with thoughts and feelings and sensations as the glitter that is swirling all around. Every time you do anything, the snow globe gets shaken. An argument with a friend will make the glitter swirl, and so will something exciting, like winning a game or getting asked out. As the glitter starts to swirl, it's much harder to clearly see the scene in front of you.

How can you get the glitter in the snow globe—or the thoughts and emotions in your mind—to settle so that you can see clearly? You need some stillness, which is exactly what mindfulness provides. Remember also that when the glitter settles, it doesn't go away; it just no longer distorts the clear view of what is in front of you.

Mindfulness Practice: The Snow Globe

- Find a snow globe, a glitter ball, or even just a jar with some water and sand or glitter, and shake it. Imagine what is floating around as your thoughts, and take a few moments to just watch as they settle. Experiment with shaking it up a lot or a little; either way, just watch and wait for it to settle.

- Now close your eyes and bring your attention to your mind. Try to imagine all of your thoughts settling with each breath. They never go away, but they can move aside and allow more clarity and calm in your own head.

You can even make your own snow globe from a kit and put your favorite inspirational images or quotes into it.

22 bringing mindfulness to your emotions

At our core, we humans have just a few basic emotions, but even these can be hard to recognize when we are feeling anxious. Take some time to explore these other emotions mindfully, in addition to exploring the mental and physical aspects of anxiety.

Exercise: What Your Emotions Feel Like

Remember a time when you felt each of these emotions. If nothing comes to mind, you might want to watch YouTube clips or listen to songs that you know make you feel these ways. Write down what you feel in your body and mind as you experience these emotions.

Emotion	What I Feel in My Body	What I Feel in My Mind
Happiness		
Sadness		
Anger		
Anxiety		

Once you start to know your body and learn to listen to its wisdom, you can start to use mindfulness of the body to ease your anxiety. This next practice is an experiment in bringing mindfulness to emotions in the body.

Mindfulness Practice: Releasing Fear

- Close your eyes and bring to mind an upcoming situation that regularly raises your anxiety level. Imagine it in your mind's eye: the people, the place, sounds, and smells.

- Now turn your attention inward, and notice where in your body you feel that stress or anxiety. Notice what these sensations feel like. Begin to imagine yourself breathing into this part of your body, just a breath at a time, slowly breathing into that spot. With each breath, breathing some calm and warmth into that area, and breathing out fear and anxiety.

- Breathing in calm…

- Breathing out worry…

- Breathing in peace…

- Breathing out fear…

You may need to try this a few times before it feels natural, or you may want to find words that fit better with your personality or the feelings you experience when you think about a difficult person, place, or thing that triggers your anxiety.

23 bringing mindfulness to everyday activities

Because we can't sit down and meditate every time something difficult comes up, we can't rely on something like a formal sitting meditation to get us through every stressful or anxious situation. It is helpful to schedule mindfulness practice for a few minutes every day, but sometimes all we have time for is to bring mindful awareness to a few moments or activities.

Here are several situations where you can experiment with being fully in the moment. Don't try to do all of them mindfully every day; just pick one or two and see if doing those mindfully can become part of your routine, and then add some more the next week.

Remember, mindfulness is essentially paying attention, so when you are doing any of these things, try to do them with your full attention and do nothing else. Think back to the story: "When we eat, we know we are eating…." Gradually, you can turn life into a mindfulness practice, and mindfulness into a way of life.

- Lying in bed when you first wake up

- Showering

- Drying yourself

- Combing or brushing your hair

- Brushing your teeth

- Making your bed

- Putting on your clothing

- Tying your shoes

- Packing your bag

- Walking

- Riding in a car or bus

- Speaking

- Listening

- Washing your hands

- Eating

- Playing sports

- Doing chores

- Cooking

- Playing music

- Stretching

- Drawing or painting

- Writing

- Playing with your pet

- Any other activities that are part of your daily routine:

_____

_____

_____

Summing Up

In this section, you learned more about the concept of mindfulness—paying attention to what is happening in the present moment with nonjudgment. Mindfulness helps with anxiety because you can see more clearly what your thoughts and feelings really are, rather than misinterpreting them. Once you see clearly, you can see what to do that will help. Staying in the moment means not being caught in worries about the future or sadness about the past, but rather appreciating and enjoying what is here, now. You also learned a few mindfulness practices and began to get to know some of your anxiety triggers and how you experience anxiety and other emotions emotionally, psychologically, and physically. In the rest of the book, we'll look at using mindfulness in some of the most challenging and anxiety-provoking situations young people face.

Take a moment now to reflect on the lessons, skills, and practices in this section.

What activity did you relate to most?

_____

_____

What skills do you think you would be most likely to use in your daily life?

_____

_____

Which skills do you think you can try in the next week?

_____

_____

This poem sums up the beauty of appreciating the present:

Ten thousand flowers in spring, the moon in autumn,
a cool breeze in summer, snow in winter.
If your mind isn't clouded by unnecessary things,
this is the best season of your life.

—Wu Men, untitled poem

At Home

Arguments. Stressed-out siblings. Rowdy roommates. Loneliness and worry. All of these and more can keep home from feeling like the comfortable place we want it to be, and that it deserves to be. Home itself might be a difficult place that triggers our anxiety, or at times we may unintentionally bring the stressors of the world home. No matter which, we cannot change everything about our environment to make home what we want it to be, but we can change a few things. And most important, we can change how we respond to challenges at home.

24 making your space peaceful

A few years back I worked with Katie, a college freshman who had terrible anxiety about being away from home and was rapidly spiraling into depression. She didn't feel close with her roommate and hated being in their room. One afternoon, I asked her to describe the room to me.

"Well," she said, "there's the dorm furniture, and my roommate has her side of the room set up, but since I never like being there and share it anyway, I just have my bed and desk and dresser on my side, with my stuff in boxes."

I was astonished. She had not put up a single poster, put any photos on her desk, or even taken her stuffed animals out of the boxes she brought with her. No wonder Katie felt so unhappy there; it didn't even feel like her room, it didn't feel like home, and it didn't feel safe!

We spent the rest of the session planning ways to set up the room so it would be a place where she could feel comfortable. After that, she strategically set up objects and art that reminded her of happy memories, put up some inexpensive curtains, and from a thrift store got a small rug and funky lamp that reflected her personality. She soon felt as though she had a calm space that was at least partly her own, away from the chaos of the world.

You might not yet be in college, but what is your space like? Does it feel safe, comfortable, yours? Those who share a room with siblings or others can even just set up small corners with objects that remind them to stay calm: perhaps some stones from the beach, photos of the mountains, candles, religious objects, inspirational quotes in calligraphy, or gifts from friends. If your home is noisy, try getting a white noise machine or turning on a fan or soft music to drown out the turmoil outside.

How can you change your environment to feel more calm and comfortable in your own home?

_____

_____

What are some objects or artwork that help you feel calm? (If you can't get the actual objects or artwork, perhaps you can get posters, postcards, or photos of them.)

_____

_____

_____

Think of inspirational quotes from books you've read, favorite song lyrics, or online posts that particularly speak to you. Write them down here, and if possible put them up somewhere you will see them regularly.

_____

_____

_____

_____

_____

25 fighting in the family

Home should feel safe and stable; that is the message we get from the media and the larger culture. But for many teens, home can feel chaotic and unpredictable, even unsafe. Parents may be fighting with each other, siblings may be struggling, and financial and other pressures can make home a tense place to be. But the fact is, we *have* to spend time there, so how can we find internal stability in the face of swirling stress and chaos?

One of my favorite visualization meditations is called the Lake Meditation. By practicing this meditation, we can stay as calm as the bottom of a lake, no matter what is happening around us. The weather and seasons may change, and we may even look different on the surface at different times, but we can remain settled deep down.

Mindfulness Practice: Lake Meditation

- This meditation can be done in almost any position, though you may find it most helpful to lie down, perhaps with a cushion beneath you.

- Take a moment to bring your attention to the sensations of your body settling into the softness beneath you.

- Now imagine a lake. Perhaps this is a place where you have spent time, or maybe one you have seen in pictures. Just imagine the water resting in the earth, the way you are resting in the cushions beneath you.

- Consider the surface of the lake, imagining the ways it changes depending on the time of day or the season—still and reflective in the morning as fog lifts off the surface, or perhaps there are some ripples in the afternoon. And though the surface may change, underneath, deep down at the bottom, the water is still.

- As the weather changes, the surface may change. Thousands of raindrops may beat down on the surface, or the sun may warm the first few inches, or wind may create waves and small whitecaps on the top of the lake. Yet underneath, there is stillness.

- Seasons change, and in this way the lake's surface changes as well. The reflection one day may be a summer sky and clouds, and then soon golden leaves fall on the surface of the lake, as the trees reflect bright autumn colors in place of summer green. As winter approaches, the surface may reflect the drab surroundings, until finally it freezes over with ice, then snow atop the ice. Even as springtime comes and the ice and snow begin to melt and the sky brightens, through it all the bottom of the lake remains still, resting, calm.

- And so while the outside world may change with time and situations that you encounter, these need not disturb the stillness, peace, and quiet underneath. Can you find the stillness deep inside of yourself, allowing yourself to rest there and ease your anxiety and worries?

- Take the lake's wisdom and lie down now for the next few minutes with strength and stillness through whatever arises around you and within you.

26 mindfulness through music

Listening to music is a great coping technique for many teens and adults. We all have our favorite songs, and just as a lullaby can calm a frightened baby, one of our favorite tunes can instantly bring us a moment of peace, calming our minds and bodies. Sometimes, though, we are too agitated to just let music calm us down. It can help to listen more deeply, more mindfully to the music, and allow its effects to calm us.

Mindfulness Practice: Mindfulness and Music

- Find a quiet space to listen to your stereo, or better yet, put on headphones.

- Make yourself comfortable lying down or sitting in an upright yet relaxed position. Make sure your clothing is comfortable and you feel warm enough.

- Take a few breaths and allow your body and mind to settle.

- There are a few ways to bring your deliberate attention to the music. One way to start is to pick a single instrument or sound to follow through the song. Listening like this can be quite soothing, as it narrows your attention, moving it away from difficult subjects. Experiment with listening to the other instruments, and see how many different sounds and tracks you can trace throughout the length of the song. You may be surprised at how much you notice.

What did you notice when following just one instrument?

_____

_____

_____

A second way of listening in a mindful manner is by listening with your body. Get comfortable, and pay attention to the sensations in your body as the sounds of the song resonate through your body. It can be amazing to see how our bodies receive and respond to music as it lands and ripples through us.

What sensations did you become aware of in your body?

_____

_____

_____

What, if anything, surprised you or interested you?

_____

_____

_____

The last way I suggest listening to music is by focusing on the body, then tracking your reactions through the song. Notice what happens automatically: emotions, memories, thoughts, or associations. As each comes up, simply notice it, name it, and return to noticing.

What emotions did you notice?

_____

_____

activity 26 ✳ mindfulness through music

What memories?

_____

_____

What other thoughts or associations?

_____

_____

Earlier you learned mindfulness of breathing, because wherever you are, you always have your breath. Now with electronic devices that fit in our pockets, we can also have mindfulness of music just about everywhere we go.

alone time 27

I once heard someone say, "If your mind is a dangerous neighborhood, don't go there alone." Those are certainly wise words, but life often has moments when we are left alone. The house is empty, our friends or our roommates are nowhere to be found, and we are left with ourselves and our own thoughts. Some people thrive on this alone time and need it to recharge mentally and emotionally. But eventually, we all become lonely. Human beings evolved to thrive in communities, with friends and families, and loneliness can be extremely painful and overwhelming.

What are some ways you deal with alone time?

_____

_____

What are some activities you do best alone?

_____

_____

What are some times you have been alone without feeling lonely or anxious?

_____

_____

_____

What are the loneliest times of day or loneliest places for you?

_____

_____

When, if at all, do you expect to be alone in the week ahead?

_____

_____

_____

Mindfulness practices like the following one can help with loneliness.

Mindfulness Practice: The Compassionate Friend

- Find a comfortable position; a sitting posture is probably best for this practice. Close your eyes. Place both hands so that you can feel their warmth on your chest. Notice what this feels like, and just gently breathe in this position.

- Now imagine you are in a room where you feel safe and cozy. It could be a room where you've been, or maybe a luxurious place in your imagination. The lighting and temperature are just right, and the furniture is soft and comfortable.

- In a moment, a visitor will come to your room, a being who would just like to be with you for a while. It may be a spiritual figure, someone from your past, a pet, or just a warm loving presence, but it should be someone who embodies qualities like courage, warmth, strength, and unconditional acceptance.

- Go to the door and invite this being in. Sitting back down, invite your friend to take a seat too, at a distance you feel comfortable with. Feel your friend's presence, and just savor what that is like. Perhaps you want to smile or otherwise acknowledge your gratitude to this person.

- And now, your compassionate friend would like to share something wise with you, to share exactly what it is you need to hear right now. Maybe it's through words, maybe it's through a gesture or an expression, or maybe it's just by transmitting a feeling; just take in whatever it is this friend wants you to know. Be together, open to anything you might hear.

- Your friend will be departing now, but you can bring his or her presence back at any time, just as you can return to feeling that nearby presence at any time and are never truly alone.

- Take a moment to reflect on what you received from this friend, and when you feel ready, gently allow your eyes to flutter open on the actual room.

What was the room like where you met your friend?

_____

_____

_____

What or whom did you pick to come visit you?

_____

_____

How did you feel in the presence of this friend?

_____

_____

What wisdom, if any, did your friend share with you?

_____

_____

_____

How did you feel right after the practice?

_____

_____

Whom else could you visualize when no one is around or get in touch with if you feel lonely?

_____

_____

calming your mind for sleep

You know the feeling: lying in bed, tossing and turning and unable to sleep. You're trying not to think about how tired you will be or to check your phone every few minutes to see what time it is. Your thoughts are racing; maybe with excitement or with nothing interesting at all, but more likely with worries. Worries in particular can keep us up at night, our thoughts bouncing to the past or future.

As the night goes on, you check the time and worry even more, and while you're looking at your phone, you decide to check your e-mail and Facebook. Now that's got you thinking and worrying even more, so you toss and turn for a while longer, knowing your stress and anxiety will be even worse when you are overtired tomorrow—and the vicious cycle repeats itself until sunrise.

For many of us, going to bed is the first time we let our guard down and stop distracting ourselves. Into that empty space comes a flood of thoughts and feelings, often overwhelming us. Regrets about the day, that embarrassing moment from lunchtime haunting us, and then we flip to tomorrow's to-do list and worrying about that exam. And when it's time to sleep, there is really nothing we can do about either the day behind us or the day ahead of us.

So how can we get into the present moment and slow down some of our thoughts and calm our bodies? I often recommend visualization exercises that calm the body and give the mind just enough to focus on.

Mindfulness Practice: Riding the Waves

- Begin by lying down on your back. Allow your head to be propped up enough so you can see your belly. Find something to place on your belly—maybe your hands, a pillow, a book, or a favorite stuffed animal.

- Focus on your breath, bringing it into your belly, and just notice as your belly slowly moves up and down, watching the object you chose as if it were gently bobbing on the waves of the ocean.

- When your mind wanders off, which it inevitably will, just bring it back to your belly, and focus your eyes on whatever is riding the gentle waves of the breath.

- Listen to the sounds of your breath…feel it all together…and just breathe like this for a few minutes until your breath has slowed down.

- Now turn out the light and keep your mind focused on the breath, riding the gentle waves until your mind and body have slowed.

This practice is one that can really help calm both the mind and the body together, but sometimes it can feel hard to focus that much. If you find that to be true for you, I'd recommend doing more to calm just the body, through this next practice.

Mindfulness Practice: Progressive Muscle Relaxation

This practice will start again with the body, slowing and relaxing your body so that it triggers your mind to relax as well. This is a practice you might read first, then try; you'll probably get the idea pretty quickly. If you want to, you can record yourself speaking aloud, or trade recordings with a friend or someone else.

- Start by lying down on your back and allowing your body to sink into the surface underneath you. Bring your attention to your breath, taking a deep breath in and feeling your belly rise, and then release.

- Squeeze all the muscles in your feet, flexing them forward and curling your toes. Notice what all that tension feels like running through your muscles. Keep squeezing just a bit harder…harder…and then release. Let go, and feel the tension ebb away and the relaxation flow into your feet and toes. Take a moment to appreciate the difference before and after you released the tension.

- Now pull your feet toward the tops of your calves and stretch the toes outward…then release. As the tension flows away, feel the newfound relaxation flow in through your feet and toes.

- On the next breath, tense the muscles of your ankles and calves for a breath or two, then relax and release, opening to the change of sensations.

- And now when you feel ready, tense the muscles of your thighs and knee for a moment or two; then when you are ready, just let go and allow the relaxation to wash over your whole lower body.

- On the next breath, clench your buttocks and hips, squeezing as tightly as you can, and then release.

- Now turn your attention to your back. Feel it tightening as your shoulders pull back and the muscles along your spine tense…and then let go.

- Next clench the muscles in your stomach and upward into your chest, your whole torso tightening for a few moments and then just letting go.

- On the next breath, turn your attention to your hands, balling them into fists as tightly as you can, squeezing and then just releasing and relaxing.

- Follow your awareness now into your forearms, holding the muscles tightly, tensing your biceps and triceps. When you do let go, just be with the feeling of relaxation as it washes back into your arms.

- On the next breath, tense your shoulders and neck, aware of what the tension feels like, and as you let go, be aware of that feeling of release.

- Finally, bring awareness to the muscles of your face. Start by furrowing your brow, then squeezing your eyes and clenching your jaw, feeling the strain and stress in all of these facial muscles, really feeling these last few moments of tension in your muscles. Then just let go, allowing the relaxation in, and just rest with it, enjoying it for a few moments.

- Take just a moment now to quickly scan all the muscles of your body. Feel the newfound relaxation in your feet and legs, up through your hips and into your torso and back; feel the relaxation in your arms and hands, and pay particular attention to it in your neck and shoulders, then in the muscles of your face. Stay with those feelings for a few more moments as you lie there.

- If you feel like it, shift to a comfortable sleeping position, focus on the relaxation seeping into your mind, and allow yourself to just drift off to sleep.

Other tips from sleep experts include turning your clock around so you can't see it, which can mean plugging your phone in somewhere other than your bedside table. Don't play with your phone for at least a half hour before bed, and definitely don't check it in the middle of the night, even to see what time it is. It may sound crazy not to know what time it is if you are tossing and turning, but think about it: doesn't knowing the time actually make you more anxious rather than less? Exercise helps, and so does eating on a regular schedule, but don't do either within at least a few hours of bedtime, and definitely stay away from caffeine and sugar. A regular bedtime ritual or routine trains your body to know when it's time to relax and get to sleep. Take a bath or shower, pray or meditate if you do those things, and read something calming like poetry or something that doesn't remind you of your stressors. If you need to, consider using an eye mask and ear plugs to keep out extra distractions. Finally, try to think of your bed as the place where you sleep, not the place where you study or catch up on e-mail or surf the Internet.

Summing Up

Home is wherever we may make it, but for some of us, home may be more triggering than relaxing. We can make some changes to our environment so that we feel safer and less anxious, but often we also need to make some changes within ourselves and make an effort to notice the positive. This section offered practices for staying calm when the house feels hectic; whether your parents are fighting or there are other worries in the home, you can remain stable and maybe even serene. Other exercises were designed to help you sleep, let go of worries, and tolerate being alone. Home also offers a number of opportunities for informal mindfulness practice, bringing mindful attention to chores, family interactions, and other activities we tend to do on autopilot.

Take a moment now to reflect on the lessons, skills, and practices in this section.

Which activity did you relate to most?

_____

_____

What skills do you think you would be most likely to use in your daily life?

_____

_____

Which skills do you think you can try in the next week?

_____

_____

The following poem describes a way to feel comfortable with ourselves, the home we will always have and always take with us.

> This being human is a guest house.
> Every morning a new arrival.
> A joy, a depression, a meanness,
> some momentary awareness comes
> as an unexpected visitor.
> Welcome and entertain them all!
> Even if they're a crowd of sorrows,
> who violently sweep your house
> empty of its furniture,
> still, treat each guest honorably.
> He may be clearing you out
> for some new delight.
> The dark thought, the shame, the malice,
> meet them at the door laughing,
> and invite them in.
> Be grateful for whoever comes,
> because each has been sent
> as a guide from beyond.

—Rumi, "The Guest House"

At School

For many young people, school is a minefield of people, places, and situations that can trigger anxiety at any time. With mindfulness, we can learn to anticipate those dangers before they arise, and then to prevent anxiety from overwhelming us.

29 mindful planning

The first step is getting to know what triggers you most during the school week. Often there's a day or two that brings up more anxiety than the rest. For many, it's Monday, knowing that the whole week is ahead; for others, it might be Friday when, for example, they have a math quiz every week, or they start talking to people about weekend plans.

What days of the week are particularly hard for you?

_____

_____

On a scale from 1 to 5, how anxious do you feel on those days?

_____

What do you tend to worry about?

_____

_____

There are also times of day that may be more stressful: a class that is particularly challenging or with a tough teacher; a gym class with a bully; or lunchtime, with the social stress of finding your friends in the cafeteria. Some people might get tired and feel more vulnerable by afternoon, and for others, medication side effects may kick in at certain times.

What times of day are harder for you?

_____

_____

On a scale from 1 to 5, how anxious do you feel during those times?

_____

What kinds of worries come up in your mind and in your body?

_____

_____

School presents a number of situations and scenarios that anyone with anxiety might dread. For some, it's tests that cause the most anxiety; for others, it may be speaking in class for a presentation or even just adding to a discussion. Maybe for you it's talking with a teacher, dealing with writer's block, or just the whole idea of school altogether.

What situations in school trigger you the most or have triggered you in the past?

_____

_____

On a scale from 1 to 5, how anxious do you feel during those times?

_____

What kinds of worries come up in your mind and in your body?

_____

_____

By now you probably have a sense of what some of your anxiety triggers are during the school day. Remember, knowing is half the battle, so armed with this knowledge, you can start to work on your anxiety as it arises in specific situations.

30 school phobia

Just going to school can cause tremendous anxiety for some teens. There are so many aspects of the day that can be overwhelming. You might want to avoid school altogether, or your body might be sending you danger signals.

I worked with a young woman named Amanda, who had a lot of stress and anxiety about school. She was a bit of a perfectionist, and that made her even more anxious about school. We talked a lot about the most stressful parts of her week and were able to identify a few specific triggers, but it was still hard for her to put her finger on exactly what it was about school that was most challenging.

After she talked to her friends and family about when she seemed the most stressed, she realized that her anxiety about the school week would begin on Sundays. Stomachaches and worrying would keep her up on Sunday nights, and she'd wake up a wreck on Monday mornings, after tossing and turning all night.

We worked out some plans to make Sunday a day to look forward to—cooking, a yoga class, and a bath in the evening all made Sundays better—but some anxiety still lingered. Monday mornings could still be hard, especially on the walk to school. In our conversations about what her Monday mornings were like, we discovered that the walk to school was one of the best opportunities for Amanda to practice mindfulness.

We are so often doing something else while we walk that we hardly notice what is happening around us, or even how we got to where we ended up. Like many other adults, I'm guilty of this. I listen to music or podcasts, I text or talk to friends, I daydream, and before I know it I'm at my destination with almost no memory of the walk itself. And yes, I too have walked straight into a tree while I was texting!

Maybe walking isn't always so interesting, but you can start to make it interesting *and* do something for your anxiety on the way to school that will get you ready to begin your day calmly and with confidence.

Mindfulness Practice: Walking Mindfully

- Find some space for walking. It can be outdoors or indoors, but make sure you have at least ten or twelve feet so that you can turn around after a few steps.

- Begin by standing up straight, with your legs about hips width apart.

- Focus your eyes on the ground in front of you.

- Take a deep breath or two, allowing your body to settle.

- Spend a moment or two making small adjustments in your posture until you feel balanced and upright.

- Feel your feet making contact with the ground.

- Slowly, just lift the heel of your right foot, being aware of all the sensations in your foot, ankle, and leg, aware of the muscles moving.

- Raise your foot, lift it into the air, and place it on the ground in front of you, taking a complete step.

- Remain aware now, as your balance shifts and weight moves into that right foot and your left foot begins to lift up. Again, be aware of all the muscle movements in your legs and entire body as you shift that leg forward and place your foot on the ground in front of you, feeling it land.

- Take a few more steps like this, aware of all the sensations of lifting, stepping, and shifting. Try to keep your mind focused and aware of the sensations of movement, weight, and balance that your body creates as you move mindfully.

- See if you can notice that moment when your balance and weight shift from one leg to the other.

Try practicing mindful walking for about five or ten minutes. You might find your mind starting to wander. Remember that your mind wandering is completely normal and to be expected. Whenever you do get distracted, just notice where your mind went and what brought it there, and gently return your attention to your walking, maybe adding in or experimenting with one of these variations:

- See if you can walk as silently as possible.

- Imagine walking on ice.

- Imagine walking while balancing a bucket of water on your head.

- Try speeding up or slowing down.

- Try to sync your breath with your movement.

How are you feeling now in your body? Do you notice any changes in how you feel?

_____

_____

How are you feeling in your mind?

_____

_____

Did any thoughts or distractions come up? What were they?

_____

_____

_____

When else could you use mindful walking (for example, in the hallway between classes, or on the way to other places)?

_____

_____

One well-known meditation teacher recommends saying something to yourself with each step; for example, repeating "Nothing to do…nowhere to go…no one to be" with every step forward.

You might also try just counting your steps and beginning over if you find yourself distracted. This suggestion is not to make the practice more frustrating, but just to help you focus more clearly on the task at hand.

Set an amount of time or distance to walk mindfully a few times a week. Maybe it's the first three blocks of the walk to school or the bus stop, or maybe it's the length of one song you are listening to. When you are done with mindful walking, just check back in with yourself physically and emotionally, and go on with your day.

You can walk mindfully in school, but try to maintain an awareness of your surroundings. Being aware can mean fewer surprises than when you keep your eyes down; you will be prepared for difficult run-ins because you can see them coming from afar.

Walking can also be a time to bring your awareness to the beauty of your surroundings, and to what is going right in your life, all of which can start to affect your attitude over time. Research has shown that paying attention to the positive when walking can give you a boost in mood. While it's true that we can't change our outlook overnight, we can start to shift things in a more positive direction.

I discussed this with Julia, a student who had practiced walking to school mindfully while noticing the beauty around her for a few months. The late summer and fall was wonderful; she focused on the warm sun, the smell of freshly mowed grass, and the beauty of the changing trees. But then winter arrived, and the world was dreary on her walk to school. Together, we tried to come up with a creative way to deal with the challenge of finding beauty in the snowy and cold world.

A few days after our conversation, I got an e-mail from Julia, with a link to a website. She had begun a blog where she posted photographs from her phone of beautiful and colorful things she had encountered on her walk to school: ice melting on a red winter berry, bright green pine needles resting against the snow, a piece of yellow yarn stuck in the leafless branches of a tree. These were all signs of life and beauty in a world that seemed lifeless if you weren't looking closely, and her walk no longer seemed so drab.

On your walk or ride to school, are there some particularly beautiful spots? A favorite tree, a flowering bush, a nest of birds?

_____

_____

_____

staying calm in the classroom

Okay, so you've gotten to school, navigated the hallway, and gotten yourself to class. Halfway through class, looking around, you realize that you missed the last few minutes of the teacher's lecture. The other students look as though they understand everything perfectly, and suddenly your body feels tense and the worry starts to kick in.

Sometimes, your anxiety can build as you are sitting in class. Any number of the short practices in this book can help. Some, like focusing on your feet or tuning into your five senses, you can do without anyone even knowing. At other times you need a little more to focus on, like reciting a few words to yourself to bring the anxiety back down.

Mindfulness Practice: Breathing In, Breathing Out

Before you begin this practice, think about how you usually feel in class in your body and mind. Then think about how you *want* to feel in your body and mind.

Now, on each in-breath, breathe in what you want to feel. On each out-breath, breathe out what you don't want to feel. For example, if you want to feel calm, relaxed, and at ease, and not agitated, stressed, and restless, just try to say those words as you breathe:

- Breathing in, I breathe in calm…

- Breathing out, I breathe out agitation…

- Breathing in, I breathe in relaxation…

- Breathing out, I breathe out stress…

- Breathing in, I breathe in ease…

- Breathing out, I breathe out restlessness…

Try just repeating these simple meditations along with your breath a few times, and see if it helps. Write them down elsewhere to save for later, or record them on your phone. If you feel self-conscious, you could just write down the key words rather than the whole meditation.

32 approaching teachers and other adults

As a shy kid, Josh struggled academically, in part because approaching teachers for extra help or explanations was difficult for him. When I was Josh's age, this was hard for me as well. Unfortunately, shy people and those who get nervous around adults miss out on important opportunities and relationships that could really help them through difficult situations, even if it's just getting extra help in school.

When I met with Josh, he described slinking out of class to avoid talking to his teacher, which meant that he never got feedback about what he was doing well or what he could improve. He did his work, but sometimes he would be unclear on the instructions and so would end up being marked down for not following directions.

Josh was eventually able to start using diaphragmatic breathing, or belly breathing, to bring the anxiety in his body and his mind under control, especially in interactions with adults. One of the main things he liked about belly breathing was that after just a bit of practice, he could do it anywhere without anyone else having to know he was doing it—a bit of "stealth mindfulness," as he called it.

Mindfulness Practice: Diaphragmatic Breathing

When we are anxious, we tend to breathe into our chests and not get the oxygen we need to really thrive and have our bodies and brains functioning at their best. Try breathing into your belly for a few minutes at first, and see if you can work your way up to five or ten minutes. The 7/11 breath is one easy way to remember how to breathe deeply: you simply breathe in for a silent count of seven, and out for a count of eleven.

- Find a comfortable upright position, either standing or sitting. Allow your body to feel a sense of uplift from the base of your spine through your chest and up into your shoulders, neck, and head.

- You can leave your eyes open and rest your gaze on the floor in front of you, or you can close them gently, whichever feels most comfortable for you.

- Gently place one hand on your chest and one hand on your belly, and bring your awareness to the sensations of your breath in those two places. You might notice that you can feel your breath more in your belly or in your chest.

- See if you can slowly shift your breath so that you are breathing from your belly rather than your chest. If this is hard, just try to shift the breath gently downward.

- Notice how you are feeling in your mind and in your body.

This practice might take effort at first, but you will soon feel comfortable with it, and eventually you won't have to use your hands. When you are approaching a teacher or trying to stay calm during an interaction with another adult in school, you can always shift your breath back into your belly, and no one even has to know what you are doing. If you start to feel overwhelmed in other circumstances, try to just check back in with a few diaphragmatic breaths.

33 class presentations

The comedian Jerry Seinfeld once said, "According to most studies, people's number one fear is public speaking. Number two is death. Death is number two. Does that sound right? This means to the average person, if you go to a funeral, you're better off in the casket than doing the eulogy!"

If you get nervous about speaking in front of crowds, you are definitely not alone. Public speaking is like many other skills. Most people are not born good at it; they get that way through practice, lots of it, in order to look as though they are speaking in a way that is completely natural and spontaneous.

When you're standing in front of your classmates, or even when you think about standing up there, remember that your anxious body is reacting to the room full of people the same way your long-ago ancestors reacted when they were staring down a group of predators. Mindfulness practices can transform our outlook so our bodies and minds are reacting to a crowd of classmates, not a crowd of saber-toothed cats: that is to say, reacting to the reality of the situation in front of us.

So how can we get better at public speaking? We can prepare in advance, and we can prepare in the moment. We don't want to get ourselves worried and, in the moment before we are there, visualize catastrophes, but we do want to be prepared. So practice, if possible. As before any big moment, sleep well, eat well, and get your body and mind in shape.

I have a friend who is a well-known professor at Harvard. He hates public speaking, and do you know what professors have to do? A lot of public speaking! He is comfortable enough with students that he can tell them how nervous he is at the start of the semester. You might not feel that comfortable with your audience, and it might not be a good idea in every setting.

But, like clockwork, my friend goes to the gym right before class, takes a shower, does a few minutes of meditation, and then heads off to class. He says he is still a bit nervous, but he is so much more able to deal with it when he's prepared himself mentally and physically. So I'd strongly recommend doing what you can before it comes time to speak.

What about when the big moment arrives? That science presentation has finally come due, and the big day is upon you. You got up, went for a run, ate a good breakfast, practiced, and maybe even did some visualization, deep breathing, or meditation.

Now you're standing in front of your class. What tends to happen to you when you speak? I know that I start speaking way too fast when I get up to talk in front of a crowd, so I write in big block letters at the top of every page SLOW DOWN. To help me keep on track and stay calm, I even write BREATHE HERE every so often. But when my body starts shaking, what really helps is focusing on my feet. That's right. I take a breath and follow my breathing all the way down into my feet, imagining them rooted in the ground, and I think about the sensations happening in the bottoms of my feet.

Try this now, and you can do a shorter version, or other variations, once you've practiced and are up there in front of the crowd.

Mindfulness Practice: Being Mindful of Your Feet

- Sitting or standing, make sure that your feet are flat on the floor underneath you.

- Take a deep breath or two.

- On your next deep in-breath, follow your awareness down into the bottoms of your feet, becoming aware of them as if for the first time, giving them all your attention.

- Feel the sensation of your body's weight resting on your feet.

- Breathe all the way into your feet, feeling the space around your feet and between your toes.

- Visualize the muscles, holding you upright. Feel the muscles in your ankles making tiny movements to hold you upright and steady.

- Feel the temperature of your feet.

- Visualize the bones of your feet, as flat as they can be.

- Feel the sensation of your socks. Are they soft? Warm? Itchy?

- Be aware of the sensation of your shoes. Bouncy? Firm? Rough?

- Be aware of the surface of the floor. Hardwood? Soft carpet? Sticky linoleum? Is it still, or can you feel vibrations?

- Feel your feet pressing down. Push your feet down into the floor, as if you can feel roots growing downward, making you stable like a tree.

- Take another moment or two to breathe all the way into your feet…and all the way out from your feet.

- Send some gratitude and appreciation to your feet.

Whenever you start to feel anxiety, just breathe down into your feet, pressing downward, rerooting yourself in the earth.

How are you feeling now in your mind and body?

_____

_____

Did any thoughts or distractions come up? What were they?

_____

_____

Which aspects of this practice did you like best? Least?

_____

_____

The aspects that were most soothing are the ones you can focus on the next time you are standing up in front of a crowd.

test anxiety 34

Tests are one of the most stressful things about school, and they are something you will continue to face well into adulthood if you go to college or graduate school or get a job that requires you to pass a licensing exam. So while tests are unlikely to go away, you can learn to manage your test anxiety and even effectively channel that nervous energy into performance.

If you experience test anxiety, it is almost as if your body interprets the test as an imminent danger. Your muscles tense up, and you can't think clearly, no matter how much you've studied, and so you freeze up or answer quickly without thinking, just to get something onto that blank page staring up at you.

Think of a test you got anxious about. What happened in your mind and body?

_____

_____

What helped you get through it?

_____

_____

Think about a time a test went well. Describe that situation, how you felt, how your body felt, and what your mind was like.

_____

_____

_____

_____

Exercise: Preparing for Stressful Events

There are all kinds of ways we can prepare our minds and bodies for stressful events like tests. Read these suggestions, then put a star next to the ones you already do and a check next to the ones you could try. Use the blank lines to add your own ideas.

- Make a study schedule.

- Study in advance to avoid cramming the night before.

- Eat a healthy dinner the night before.

- Get a good night's sleep the night before.

- Avoid too much caffeine or other substances.

- Eat a healthy breakfast in the morning.

- Wear comfortable clothing.

- Get some exercise before the exam. (Studies have shown that even light exercise can boost test scores, so you might try a jog around the school or up and down the stairs during a test break.)

- Meditate or focus on your breath.

- Visualize success.

- Give yourself a pep talk, or give your friends a pep talk.

- Listen to calming music.

- Watch a funny video or listen to a funny podcast.

- _____

- _____

- _____

Once you are in the room with the test, there are a few more things you can do. First of all, waiting for the tests to be handed out can be unbearable, so that is the perfect time to use some of your mindfulness skills. Focus on your breath as you wait, and each time you notice your mind wandering into the future or the past, gently bring it back to the sensation of your breath. Try this, or use some deep breathing you learned earlier, as you wait for the tests to go around. Ideally, you want to have a level of anxiety that keeps you focused and alert, but not so much that you can't think straight.

Try the next practice. It can help you stay focused and calm when you are actually taking a test.

Mindfulness Practice: Counting Sounds

Right now, just take a moment to become aware of all the sounds in the room. You might even want to close your eyes. If you have trouble noticing all the sounds in the silence, start with sounds nearest to you, and gradually work your way outward. Try this for about a minute, writing down the sounds as you notice them.

How do you feel after trying this practice?

_____

_____

How is the anxiety in your mind and in your body?

_____

_____

Now that you've tried that for a minute, let's do a variation. Write down the sounds again for another minute, except this time, also write down what emotions, thoughts, urges, or memories you associate with each sound. Return just to listening, and then to the test. Here's an example: *I can hear the clock ticking. It reminds me how little time I have and is making me more stressed. Okay, I'll lean back and take a breath to clear my mind, then dive back into the work.*

_____

_____

_____

_____

_____

Now that you've practiced this exercise for a few minutes, try this simple variation the next time you are feeling stressed out. Just notice three, five, or ten sounds in whatever situation you are in, and see how much your mind and body change, settle down, and become more focused.

Try this the next time you are in a test situation. Simply lean back in your chair, close your eyes, notice five sounds, and then lean in again and go back to your work. You can write the sounds down or not, but just noticing them and then coming back to what you need to focus on will make your mind a little sharper and your body a little more relaxed.

In his book *On Writing*, Stephen King writes: "The scariest moment is just before you start. After that, things can only get better." Yes, even the master of horror is afraid of the blank page!

As you may have guessed, the person writing this book is, well, a writer. And like most writers, I've suffered from writer's block for hours, days, in fact probably even weeks when you add up all the time. Writer's block happens to everyone, even the most creative of people.

There is no quick way to overcome writer's block; if someone had found one, that person would be a millionaire and the world's most prolific writer. Still, mindfulness can help get the creative juices flowing.

In a way, this practice is a variation on noticing sounds. Rather than noticing sounds, we are noticing sensations in our bodies. This can get us out of our heads, where our thoughts are blocked up, and into our bodies, where we may find a little more creativity and comfort.

Mindfulness Practice: Counting Sensations

- Sit up straight and take a few deep, mindful breaths.

- Now bring your attention to your body, quickly scanning from your feet up to your head and becoming aware of any sensations in your body.

- Pay attention now to sensations deep inside your body, as well as tactile sensations on the surface of your skin.

- Notice your body temperature and any subtle movements your body might be making unconsciously.

Write down five sensations:

_____

_____

_____

_____

_____

How are you feeling now in your mind and body?

_____

_____

Try the exercise again, this time noticing any thoughts or emotions that arise with the sensations, and then return your attention to your body.

1. When I felt _____ in my body, I thought _____
    and I felt this emotion: _____.

2. When I felt _____ in my body, I thought _____
    and I felt this emotion: _____.

3. When I felt _____ in my body, I thought _____
    and I felt this emotion: _____.

4. When I felt _____ in my body, I thought _____
    and I felt this emotion: _____.

5. When I felt _____ in my body, I thought _____
    and I felt this emotion: _____.

Now try brainstorming some ideas for your writing, maybe inspired by this exercise, or maybe just opened up by the space in your mind.

Write your ideas here:

_____

_____

_____

_____

_____

_____

36 cafeteria concerns

It has become a cliché in movies about school life: a kid walks into the cafeteria, scans the room, sees nothing but tables full of unfriendly faces or with no empty seats, and starts to panic. It's a cliché for good reason—most of us have been there, and it's a scenario that most of us dread.

Mindfulness Practice: A CALM Reminder

This practice offers a quick and easy way to calm down when panic sets in in this kind of situation. All you have to remember is CALM: **c**hest, **a**rms, **l**egs, **m**ovements and mind. You can do it standing up, sitting or lying down, or in whatever position you are in when you get worked up.

- Stand up tall and take a breath.

- First scan your chest. Does it feel tight? Is the breath shallow and stuck here? Lift and open the chest, creating enough room for your heart and lungs. Be aware of the rhythm of the pumping heart and expanding lungs opening further with each breath.

- On the next breath, quickly scan your arms. Lift and drop your shoulders once, and allow your arms to dangle. Now scan upward from the hands through the forearms and upper arms. Do you detect any tension? If so, can you gently let it go? Be aware of sensations and urges, and just breathe with these.

- On the next breath, direct your attention to your legs, allowing your attention and breath to flow through your feet…your calves…your thighs. Do you feel jumpy or shaky in the legs? Gently try to make them still. Feel yourself grounded, strong and solid on the floor beneath you, which is holding you upright.

- Next, bring your attention to your whole body, to any slight movements your body is already making or adjustments you would like to make to be more comfortable. Then bring your attention to your mind, just noticing your thoughts and allowing them to settle.

When you quickly brought your attention to these parts of the body, what did you notice?

_____

_____

What did your physical sensations tell you about your emotional state?

_____

_____

Describe any physical adjustments you made that shifted how you felt emotionally.

_____

_____

Summing Up

This section was written to help you get to school, be in school, and approach a number of different school-related situations by using mindfulness practices to reduce and manage your anxiety from the classroom to the cafeteria. Hopefully the exercises and tips in this section have been helpful to you in thinking about the best way to handle school-related anxiety.

Take a moment now to reflect on the lessons, skills, and practices in this section.

Which activity did you relate to most?

_____

_____

What skills do you think you would be most likely to use in your daily life?

_____

_____

Which skills do you think you can try in the next week?

_____

_____

In the Social World

Our friends are supposed to make our lives richer and fuller, and they usually do. But they can sometimes make life more stressful. Friendships are full of everything from petty drama to serious challenges, as well as laughter and fun. Parties are supposed to be times to unwind and celebrate, but for many they are times of greater stress and anxiety. Many of us do not like conflict, and so we avoid it at all costs. Dating can be exciting and fun, but can bring unwanted pressures. And while the greatest rewards of friendship are found in listening to and supporting a friend, sometimes a friend's struggles can feel like too much for one person to handle. Not to mention the fact that at least half of our social interactions are online, with no way to judge people's facial expressions or tone of voice. No wonder there is so much to be anxious about in our social lives!

All of these concerns are completely normal, and you are definitely not the only one feeling awkward, anxious, or alone in these areas. But some people get more anxious than others in social situations, to the point that they start avoiding social events. This avoidance can begin to have a negative impact on their relationships and their ability to achieve important goals.

Things may or may not be that bad for you, but the fact is that many teens struggle with social anxiety, and most are looking for something that can help with the discomfort. Mindfulness can give you more confidence and help you stay calm in those interpersonal encounters that can really set off the panic alarm.

37 your social anxiety triggers

Socializing may seem to come naturally to some of your peers. Often, they have just had better role models or gotten more practice. The fact is, the best way of getting over shyness and social phobia is to practice by placing yourself in social situations. The more you do it, the easier it becomes, just like learning an instrument or a sport. Unfortunately, the reverse is also true; the more you avoid social situations, the more you fall behind in social skills, and the less confidence you have. The less confidence you have, the less you socialize, and the worse your anxiety gets. Of course, approaching what we fear isn't easy, but it's never too late to reverse that trend, and start to approach, rather than avoid.

You don't have to be perfect right away; you can work up to feeling *more* comfortable at the next party, next month's prom, or whatever the next big social event in your life is. If a big party is weeks away, you have weeks to hone your skills, and plenty of people to practice small talk with before you go up against the greats: the people you want to be friends with or perhaps someone you have a crush on. And if time is short, mindfulness practices can help you calm down in the moment.

Start with easy stuff for warm-ups. Keep in mind as you approach an unfamiliar group of people that you want to identify things you have in common, rather than compare differences. If you are at the same party, you already share something. Maybe you have friends in common, school in common, age in common, a favorite team in common, or a love of stale potato chips in common; these are all potential conversation starters. So if you find yourself asking, *Do I belong here?* the answer is, if you were invited, yes!

Write down some social situations that trigger your anxiety.

_____

_____

_____

_____

_____

What might be some negative consequences of avoiding those situations?

_____

_____

_____

What might be some benefits of approaching those situations?

_____

_____

_____

Mindfulness Practice: STOP the Social Panic

A short practice for entering social situations when you want to just get out of there is to STOP yourself from running away. It's a simple acronym:

- **S**top what you are doing.

- **T**ake a breath. Focus on all the sensations of the in-breath: the cold air hitting your nose and the back of your throat, moving down your throat, then your belly and diaphragm expanding as you inhale. Feel your diaphragm release now, the warm air traveling upward and out through your lips and nostrils.

- **O**bserve. What is happening right now in your external environment: what are the sounds, sights, and smells of the space around you? Now shift to your internal experience, sensations in your body, comfort or discomfort, and observing your mind: what thoughts, emotions, and images are floating through your mind?

- **P**lan and proceed. Is there a way you can bring your inner state more in line with the outer world? Are there any adjustments you can make to your outer world to help it align with your inner world? Are there any actions you can take at this moment to improve the situation?

Try this practice now.

Write down any upcoming social events where you can imagine using STOP.

_____

_____

_____

At parties or other gatherings, how could you find a few seconds to check in by using STOP?

_____

_____

Keeping your social calendar well balanced is another way to help yourself. Set good boundaries; don't say yes to every event—or no to every event either. Go to those you most want to go to, and also a few that challenge you. Be careful not to double book yourself; this can be hard if you are anxious about saying no, or suffer from FOMO (fear of missing out), but you'll feel even more stressed and anxious if you're rushing from one place to the next. Remember to take time off from socializing on some weekends or afternoons.

It can be tempting to become perfectionistic about social interactions, which are, in reality, impossible to control. Don't expect the party or the date or the hangout to go exactly the way you plan it or want it to; chances are it won't, and your expectations might be disappointments waiting to happen. But do think about what part you can play to help social situations go well; after all, your behavior and reactions are the only things you can hope to have any control over. And remember, social events are about enjoying yourself, so try to have fun as you practice the strategies in this section.

38 dealing with difficult people

What could be more anxiety provoking than difficult people? There are four general ways we tend to deal with, or not deal with, such people. We can avoid, appease, accept, or assert.

Avoidance is the strategy many people use; if you don't like particular people, simply, don't deal with them! Avoid parties or situations where you might run into them. If some obnoxious kids give you a hard time about your weight, avoid them at all costs, especially in places like the locker room. Avoidance often works and does keep us safe, but unfortunately, we cannot avoid people forever, especially in a small high school or college, where we are bound to run into the same people over and over.

Another way to deal with difficult people is to appease them—to let them do what they want so they will leave you alone. This approach can work in the short term because it keeps the peace and makes a lot of people happy. But, in the long run, appeasing can leave you feeling unhappy and resentful, and it can start a pattern in which people take advantage of you.

The healthier long-term strategies involve acceptance and assertiveness. The first involves not liking these people or their behavior, but perhaps accepting that you cannot avoid or appease them forever; and that you cannot change them, but you can change how you react to them. This does not mean you have to like particular people, but it does mean you have to accept that they exist, and there are better and worse ways to interact with them.

In the end, the best way to handle difficult people is usually through assertiveness. That means striking a balance between being a passive pushover and giving in to aggressive impulses. It means standing up for yourself, which starts with self-compassion and self-esteem. It can also mean telling people how you feel, setting good boundaries and learning to say no, or directly asking others to treat you differently. And once you have done your best, it may mean getting adults involved.

Even without bullying, simple disagreements and conflicts with others in school can flare and become overwhelming, creating anxiety and school avoidance. The following is a practice that many people find grounding, boosting their confidence as they go into difficult interpersonal situations. Try this practice in your everyday life, and then try it when you know you are walking into a situation where you might feel pushed around emotionally or physically.

Mindfulness Practice: Harnessing the Four Elements

This simple practice is easy to remember, because it involves just knowing the four elements—earth, air, water, and fire—that formed the basis of many ancient beliefs. It works best standing, although you can do it sitting down.

- First, feel your feet rooted deeply in the earth like a tree. You are making contact with earth, the first element. Earth is solid and will hold you stable. Feel the earth beneath you; you can even imagine roots burrowing deep into the earth.

- Next, feel the air at your nostrils. Air makes us free and independent. Air represents the power of our minds, blowing away our fears. Feel your chest and belly open and expand with each breath.

- Once you have connected with air, take a moment to just swallow the saliva in your mouth, and follow it into your belly. The element water flows, settles, and reflects.

- Lastly, feel the energy from deep inside your body. This is the fire of life that gives us confidence, strength, and power in the world.

- Take a moment now to connect with each element: earth with its stability, air of independence, water of reflection, and fire of life. Ask yourself whether you need more of any of these qualities as you face a challenge.

Describe how you felt after this practice.

_____

_____

_____

39 when a friend is struggling

Friendship means many things, including being ready to listen or to provide a shoulder to cry on. Friends may come to us to about a range of issues, from arguments at home and social drama to larger concerns like thoughts about sex, drugs, cutting, and other issues that even adults may find difficult to listen to. It can be hard to hear what a friend is going through, but mindfulness can help us stay steady and supportive as we listen. We need to be calm and clear in order to listen and advise our friends best.

Think about your best friends, from now and from years past. What is it that makes those people such good friends? Many people would say it is loyalty, being a good listener, supportiveness, and reliability, among other important qualities. These are often the qualities we hope we can offer to others as well.

What do you think are the qualities that make a good friend?

_____

_____

Imagine a time when you shared with and listened to a friend or a trusted person and felt completely comfortable speaking and listening. What was this experience like?

_____

_____

_____

How did your body feel during that conversation?

_____

_____

What made you feel comfortable?

_____

_____

_____

_____

We often become anxious when we worry about our friends or feel powerless to help them. Though no one may be in real danger, we react as if we might be, in part because strong emotions can be contagious. When listening to someone who is suffering, we might become anxious because we don't know what to say. Or perhaps we are anxious over sharing something about ourselves because we are afraid of being judged.

Anxiety affects each of us differently. For some people, it may lead to offering advice impulsively without considering all the consequences. For others, it may lead to holding back from sharing their best ideas. And there are times when it is probably *not* a good idea for you to speak your thoughts, or times when it is wisest to suggest that a friend seek support from an adult, a professional, or someone else who could be more helpful than you.

With mindful attention, you will be better able to see those times and watch your anxiety subside. You will know when you are really able to listen and be helpful, and really able to speak and feel confident, and when to do something else altogether. These practices will not instantly give you all the answers or make every difficult conversation easy, but they probably will lead to more productive and helpful conversations for everyone.

In many cultures, listening is valued even more highly than speaking as a sign of wisdom. Cultivating our ability to mindfully listen helps us in all our relationships, and eventually such skillful listening and wisdom become contagious, rather than our strong emotions being so contagious.

The following instructions from insight dialogue offer a way to relate and listen mindfully to others. Insight dialogue, an approach that teaches deep, mindful speaking and listening, is basically an interactive two-person meditation. It helps create the kind of trusting interaction you may have just described. The essential aspects of mindful insight dialogue are *pause, relax, trust* what will emerge, *listen* deeply, and *speak* the truth.

It may seem like a lot to keep in mind at first, but with practice, these things become easier. Following are some questions you might want to ask yourself to get into the mode of mindful listening. You can just try to remember these, or you can practice with a friend or someone you trust.

Mindful Listening

First, just bring your complete attention to the person you are with. Notice everything you can about them and their emotional state. Ask yourself:

- What does their facial expression and body language tell you?

- What are the qualities of their breath? Their voice?

- What emotions can you detect?

Now turn your attention to your own face and body, your own breath and voice.

- Can you let go of distracting thoughts?

- What emotions can you detect internally?

- How do you feel on the inside, and how might you appear on the outside?

- Can you open yourself more in any way, adjusting your mind, body, or breath to be more receptive to what this person is saying?

- As the other person speaks, do you notice yourself truly listening, or do you find yourself waiting for a turn to speak?

These are all things to consider as you begin listening mindfully to a friend. When you are able to listen in this way, you will also be able to speak from a place of wisdom where you are more likely to be helpful.

Mindful Speaking

Speaking mindfully has many of the same qualities as listening mindfully. Take a breath or two before responding. Speak from your heart, and consider the acronym THINK to speak assertively and helpfully.

- **True**: Is what I want to say **true**?

- **Helpful**: Is what I want to say **helpful**?

- **I**: Am **I** the best one to say it?

- **N**: Is it **necessary** to say it now?

- **K**: Is it **kind** to this person and others?

These questions are important to consider in weighing a response. Also remember that sometimes saying nothing, or even saying "I don't know," is not only okay, but can be the most helpful thing you can do. As the writer Margaret Lee Runbeck said, "Silence make the real conversations between friends. Not the saying, but the never needing to say that counts."

40 the pressure of parties and proms

One of the hardest things about walking into a new social situation is feeling so alone. *What if I'm the first one there? What if there is no one I know to talk to? What if my friends are busy talking to other people or leave early?* These and other questions and doubts can plague the most confident among us in the days and hours leading up to a social event and then hijack us at any moment during the event itself. How can we stay calm in the face of such worries?

At times it may look like everyone around you is comfortable and confident. But the reality is that other kids, and even adults, are often just as anxious as you are. They just might be better at hiding it or have a few tricks to handle it. Social gatherings are a good time to remember this old maxim: "Don't compare your insides to other people's outsides." Sure, people may look confident on the outside, but that doesn't mean they are. And remember, you may not feel confident, but that doesn't mean you look as nervous as you feel. The good news, and the bad news, is that most people probably just aren't paying that much attention to you.

If you do not always have some*one*, it can be helpful to have some*thing* strong and stable with you, an object to remind you of your own strength. A small, beautiful stone can serve as a reminder and is easy enough to carry in your pocket with no one ever having to know it's there. Next time you're out for a walk, keep your eyes open for a small stone or pebble. It helps if it has nice associations with a beautiful place or vacation, but this isn't necessary. Bring the pebble home and when you have time, take it out and study it.

Mindfulness Practice: A Pebble for Your Pocket

- Hold the stone in one hand, and just take a moment to study what it looks like. Notice its shape, its color, and other aspects of its appearance.

- Now close your eyes and just become aware of the stone's weight in the palm of your hand.

- Take a moment to notice other qualities—coolness or warmth, roughness or smoothness— the stone has.

- Consider how solid this stone is, how much power it has to perhaps have lasted for billions of years, and seen everything from the beginning of life on Earth to the dinosaurs to human beings today, and hardly changed at all in that time.

- Keep the stone in your pocket, and just touch it as a reminder of your own strength whenever you start to feel anxious in a social situation, allowing it to bring you back to the present moment with enduring strength.

41 talking on the phone

The digital world can connect us in incredible ways with people from all over the world, but with all the typing and texting, many of us are out of practice with face-to-face and even telephone interactions.

Like so much else in this book, using the phone without anxiety just takes practice—practice many of us do not have, so we avoid answering a call and just text back instead. Often, however, a phone call is the most appropriate way to communicate with someone, and the older you get the more important it becomes; it's unlikely that job offers will ever arrive by text message!

The easiest way to start is with brief, uncomplicated phone calls. Try calling friends and family and asking simple questions, then gradually work your way up to more complicated questions with the people who make you the most nervous. If you're worried that you're bothering people when you call, just ask, "Do you have a few minutes to talk right now?" or "Is this a good time?" and you'll have your answer right away.

Use the mindfulness and relaxation practices that you find most helpful to stay focused on the present moment. Phone calls offer built-in moments for check-ins like STOP, CALM, and mindful speaking and listening, or practices like the 7/11 breath. Each time the phone rings, you can pause before responding and feel your breath in your body; before calling, you can take a moment to scan your body or take some breaths.

Keep in mind that there are advantages to being invisible on the phone; no one can see you blush or avoid eye contact, and you can do a few things that people don't even need to see. For example, you'll sound more confident and comfortable if you're smiling, even when people can't see you; that's a common telemarketer's trick. You can also pace or walk around the room if that helps you calm down, even doing some mindful walking or stretching as you talk, or standing up confidently on a phone interview. You can also keep a hand on your belly to keep your breathing steady, or use other tricks you've learned from this book.

dating and relationships

There is little that causes us to feel crazier than romantic feelings, crushes, sex, relationships, and breakups. Roller-coaster emotions combine with hormones and peer pressure to make us feel completely overwhelmed. Movies and TV tell us we will have not just storybook endings, but also romantic-comedy beginnings and middles, with any awkward moments somehow charming. At the same time, we see that many of us have divorced parents or friends who are struggling in their relationships. All of these cultural messages are very confusing, worsening our anxiety about romance. Plus, relationships and intimacy are hard; they make us feel vulnerable, no matter how anxious or calm we might be.

Right now, close your eyes for a moment and take a few breaths, settling your body and mind. Then open your eyes, take a moment to ponder the words that follow, and write down what you observe in terms of how your body and mind react as you read each one. You might notice images, thoughts, memories, or feelings.

boyfriend

_____

_____

girlfriend

_____

_____

hookup

_____

_____

attraction

_____

_____

sex

_____

_____

relationship

_____

_____

These are *supposed* to be happy, positive words, and they often are, but just as often, we have feelings of sadness, anxiety, shame, or confusion around them. In fact, if you have any or even all of those feelings, well, congratulations—you're a human being!

So how can we deal with the anxiety of dating? For the most part, this section will cover how to deal with those people who bring up strong emotions when they are nearby: people you have feelings for and *want* to date, people who make you anxious with anticipation and excitement. But many of the ideas in this section can help you stay confident in that yucky situation when you run into those people you *used* to date, because you cannot avoid them forever.

Now comes the hard part—actually talking to that cute boy or girl in your class. You've admired them from afar for months, if not longer, and now it's time to practice working up the courage and finding the calm to look cool as you start a conversation or consider (gulp!) actually asking them out.

What automatic thoughts, emotions, and sensations come up when you think about that cute boy or girl in your class?

_____

_____

What comes up as you think about approaching them?

_____

_____

Next, we'll work toward the big goal of asking this person out. Remember, you might not get all the way there, and you still run the risk of their saying no, but basically how it works is to keep challenging yourself to be around them, and through *exposure* to them, become comfortable. What you need to do is create a hierarchy, a list of interactions with this person, working up to asking them out (or whatever your top goal might be). So you might put something like "walking past Jesse in the hallway" at zero (not anxious at all) and "asking Jesse out" at five (extremely anxious). What other situations might you put on the list? Saying hello? Friending on Facebook? Commenting on a Facebook post? Offering a compliment in person? Making small talk about the big history paper? Sitting next to this person in the cafeteria? Asking for studying advice? Calling? Texting? Asking for a hug?

Think of a few hypothetical interactions that trigger those automatic reactions above, and list them below, with zero being not at all anxious and five being the anxiety you imagine you would feel asking this person out.

_____

_____

Here are a worst-case thought, an overly perfectionistic thought, and a realistic goal for a scenario that may be like one you wrote down.

Sample scenario: *Commenting on Jesse's Facebook status*

Worst-case thought: *Everyone sees my comment and makes fun of me, it goes viral on some "dumbest Facebook posts ever" blog.*

Perfectionistic thought: *Everyone should think that everything I write on Facebook is witty and charming.*

Realistic goal: *I can take a risk and try to write something that Jesse will appreciate, and if people think it's weird or stupid, I can always delete the comment.*

Choose five of the interactions you just wrote down and come up with thoughts and goals for them. Have some fun with the worst-case and perfectionistic thoughts; yes, this is hard, but a sense of humor helps!

Scenario 1: _____

_____

Worst-case thought: _____

_____

Perfectionistic thought: _____

_____

Realistic goal: _____

_____

Scenario 2: _____

_____

Worst-case thought: _____

_____

Perfectionistic thought: _____

_____

Realistic goal: _____

_____

Scenario 3: _____

_____

Worst-case thought: _____

_____

Perfectionistic thought: _____

_____

Realistic goal: _____

_____

Scenario 4: _____

_____

Worst-case thought: _____

_____

Perfectionistic thought: _____

_____

Realistic goal: _____

_____

Scenario 5: _____

_____

Worst-case thought: _____

_____

Perfectionistic thought: _____

_____

Realistic goal: _____

_____

Hopefully that exercise was at least a little fun. Next, let's come up with some realistic thoughts to help you stay mentally grounded and some mindfulness or relaxation practices you can use if you get overwhelmed. Thinking about what has worked for you in the past can help.

Sample scenario: *Commenting on Jesse's Facebook status*

Realistic thought: *I'm going to comment on Jesse's Facebook status. A few people will probably like it, some people might not like it, and most people won't see it or won't comment.*

Calming or mindfulness practice: *7/11 breathing*

Scenario 1: _____

Realistic thought: _____

_____

Calming or mindfulness practice: _____

_____

Scenario 2: _____

Realistic thought: _____

_____

Calming or mindfulness practice: _____

_____

Scenario 3: _____

Realistic thought: _____

_____

Calming or mindfulness practice: _____

_____

Scenario 4: _____

Realistic thought: _____

_____

Calming or mindfulness practice: _____

_____

Scenario 5: _____

Realistic thought: _____

_____

Calming or mindfulness practice: _____

_____

Okay, now you're on your own to start working toward your goal (if you want to be), or you could try sharing this exercise with a trusted friend or therapist.

Keep in mind that this relationship stuff is not easy. People get nervous about it for good reason, and not every situation will go perfectly. So remember, after you try these exercises, think back to what the realistic goal for the situation was, rather than the outcome or response you got. Like everything in this book, and everything in life for that matter, this work is about progress, not perfection. That guy or girl probably won't fall in love with you immediately after your Facebook comment, but you will have taken the first step toward building your confidence, which, in the end, is the larger goal than just getting that date.

using social media 43

In recent years, the Internet has become an overwhelmingly popular place for socializing. Facebook, Twitter, and other social networking sites offer lots of opportunities for interaction—along with plenty of opportunities for social anxiety!

At the same time, technology offers amazing opportunities to practice and boost your mindfulness practice. Use Instagram to take and share photos of beautiful things on your walk to school. Start a Facebook group for your meditation practice, and get connected with other teens dealing with anxiety on Twitter, Tumblr or Reddit groups. Dozens of smartphone apps that remind you to take a breath or guide you through a meditation are just waiting for you to download and try.

All this is positive, but still, checking our news feed can put us on an emotional roller coaster. In a matter of seconds, we can go from blissful ignorance to suddenly learning that an ex is in a new relationship, a best friend is getting bullied, or a sibling is having a hard time in college—with just a click. So much information at once is a recipe for emotional overload. Many teens I talk to describe feeling anxiety and dread about checking their social media, but also worry they will miss something if they don't. This is another place where some mindful relaxation before checking in online can help, as well as maintaining your mindfulness as you spend time online.

Give yourself about five minutes to try this practice now or at some point in the next few days. You don't have to do it every time you log in, but just try it every so often.

Mindfulness Practice: Mindful Social Media

- Take a deep breath, shrug your shoulders, and allow your body to relax for a few more breaths.

- Take another breath, shrug, and allow your mind to relax.

- Log in to whatever social networking site you use most on your phone or computer. Read the first update you see, and *only* that first update. Sit back, scan your body and mind, and notice what you feel; for example, tense, tight, loose, tired, relaxed, jittery, empty, queasy, hot, cold, happy, sad, angry, jealous, resentful, left out, nothing, or something else entirely.

- Close your eyes, take another breath, and look at the next update. What comes to your body? What comes to your mind?

- Once more, close your eyes, take a breath, clear your mind, and "reset" yourself as best as you can. Read the next update.

Continue like this for a few minutes, and record below all the different emotions that came up in the time you spent reading status updates and tweets and seeing how people are doing.

_____

_____

What themes did you notice, if any?

_____

_____

Social media offers yet another opportunity to be mindful of your experience and slow down the emotional roller coaster, putting you a bit more in the driver's seat. So while it may not be realistic to do this whole practice every time you go online, I recommend a check-in, perhaps with STOP, just before and after you see what everyone else is up to.

mindful self-compassion 44

If we bring self-compassion to ourselves in those moments when we tend to get anxious around other people, a lot can change. Let's say your thoughts or feelings tell you that you're a loser, or that you would look or sound like a loser in a particular situation. Now what would happen if you brought some mindful self-compassion to this scenario? Do you have to believe those thoughts, just because they are thoughts? Does feeling like a loser really mean you're a loser?

If feeling bad or ashamed about a situation worked to make the situation better, I'd recommend it, but I have my doubts that beating yourself up on top of feeling anxious and awkward is really going to help. Instead, can you focus on your breath and clear your mind? Can you slow your breath a bit and reset the body? Can you use another practice from this book?

Describe a social situation coming up that might make you anxious.

_____

_____

_____

What thoughts or feelings come up?

_____

_____

_____

In what ways do you think others might judge you negatively?

_____

_____

What are some kinder words you can use to talk to yourself about the situation?

_____

_____

_____

_____

Summing Up

Our best moments and memories tend to be with friends, while other people may stir up anxiety and avoidance. But more than almost anything else in life, we cannot avoid people. When you have left classrooms, cafeterias, and locker rooms behind, parties, dating, and jobs will still be part of life.

Building confidence and comfort in social situations mostly just takes practice. Over time, you can learn to approach, rather than avoid, those interpersonal situations that overwhelmed you in the past. By remaining compassionate and patient with yourself and others, and focusing on realistic goals instead of perfectionism and worst-case scenarios, you will be well on your way.

Take a moment now to reflect on the lessons, skills, and practices in this section.

Which activity did you relate to most?

_____

_____

What skills do you think you would be most likely to use in your daily life?

_____

_____

Which skills do you think you can try in the next week?

_____

_____

Performing Under Pressure

The preceding three chapters of this book are divided the discussion of anxiety into neat categories: home, school, and social life. But there are a number of other situations where we can find ourselves overwhelmed with anxiety—performances, driving, and interviews, for example—that don't necessarily fit precisely into one of those categories. This chapter aims to address other times when anxiety can strike and mindfulness can help. Like the other exercises in this book, anything you read here can be used in just about any situation, so feel free to experiment with the practices, even if something like stage fright or driving phobia is not an issue for you in particular. You still may learn something useful to use in another situation that gets you anxious.

45 job and college interviews

Interviews present a unique challenge. We need to find the right balance between confidence and arrogance. We are supposed to look humble without coming across as having low-self esteem. With all this to keep in mind, plus the high stakes of wanting that job or admissions offer, we can easily end up anxious before, during, and after an interview.

But what if there were a simple way to look and also feel confident? A recent Harvard Business School study looked at whether holding your body in certain poses can affect your confidence by affecting your hormones. The researcher found that "high-power" poses lead to more of the good hormones for confidence, and fewer of the stress and anxiety hormones. The poses that work best are ones that open up the chest; for example, by standing with chest up and out, legs apart, and hands on hips, like Wonder Woman or Superman. After people practiced these poses for a few minutes before mock job interviews, interviewers perceived them as more confident and were more likely to hire them. Sounds crazy, I know. But apparently it works to transform you from worrier to warrior.

There are other tips that can also help. Remember to dress your best, allow plenty of time to get to the interview, and think ahead about the qualities and achievements you most want to get across to the interviewer. Reflect on the questions below now, and then be sure to review your answers right before an interview; it will be an instant confidence booster!

What are the best and most unique qualities about you that you want to share with the interviewer?

_____

_____

What are some things you are most proud of accomplishing in your life up to this point?

_____

_____

Mindfulness Practice: Breathing in Confidence

- Find a quiet spot to practice, maybe outside or in the bathroom or hallway before your interview. Stand upright, chest open, hands on hips.

- Turn your attention to your breath. Imagine your breath going deep into your belly and deep into your body.

- With each breath, imagine your body filling to the very edges with confidence.

- Feel the confidence radiating outward, past your skin and beyond the edges of your body.

- Now imagine walking in full of confidence and meeting the interviewer. In your mind, make solid eye contact and practice your smile, your firm handshake, and your self-assured greeting.

- Remind yourself that the people in charge already think favorably of you and are interested in you, or you wouldn't be there for the interview.

- Take one last deep breath, open your eyes, and head on in.

46 athletics

Sports are as much a mental game as a physical one, especially at the elite levels. Asked what it takes to be at the very top, Olympic and professional athletes often respond that there are far more athletes who are physically capable of competing at that level than most people realize. The difference, these elite athletes will tell you, is in the quality of the "inner" game: the mental training, toughness, and discipline that allows you to perform under pressure without choking in front of the team and the crowd, whether it's a cluster of parents or a TV audience of millions.

Physical performance takes practice, years of it, and so does mental performance. Many athletes practice slow, mindful movement to bring close attention to each tiny movement of their swing or shot. Others practice with their nondominant hand or foot to bring new awareness to their movement. Still others use visualization or practice meditation to steady their nerves and sharpen their concentration, training themselves to be alert, yet calm. Phil Jackson, who has coached the Chicago Bulls and LA Lakers to basketball championships, meditates and teaches his players the practice, and golfer Tiger Woods and his family meditate, as did famous football player Joe Namath and many other top athletes throughout history.

No matter what your sport, cross-training is critical to top performance. Boxers study ballet to stay light on their feet, basketball players become attuned to their bodies through martial arts, and divers weight train for strength. Cross-training keeps athletes nimble and in touch with their bodies, and certain cross-training can assist with calm in the face of anxiety. More and more, athletes cross-train with yoga or other movement meditations like tai chi or qigong to prepare mentally and physically for a game or performance.

Yoga does not have to mean a long class or a superheated studio, or having to bend yourself into an uncomfortable pretzel. It can mean a few moments of simple stretching with attention to the breath. As we do yoga, it can be easier to follow the breath and stay intimately connected with the body, soothing our anxiety and honing our focus. If you find yoga helpful, encourage your coach or PE teacher to incorporate it as part of mental and physical cross-training.

Give these poses a try at any time, and definitely before an athletic event you are feeling anxious about.

Mindfulness Practice: Pregame Yoga

Downward Facing Dog

This pose is very helpful in clearing the mind.

- Get down on your hands and knees. Place your knees beneath your hips and your hands straight out in front of your shoulders. Feet and hands should be about equal distance apart. Tuck your toes under and keep your fingers pointing forward and pressing into the ground.

- Exhale as you push and lift your knees away from the ground, with the knees and heels bent. Now straighten up and push your backside toward the ceiling.

- On the next exhale, push your thighs back and up and your heels down toward the floor. Keep your knees straight but unlocked, and using very small movements, try to rotate your thighs.

- Push your fingers into the floor and your shoulder blades back toward your hips. Rotate your upper arms outward as if broadening your shoulders, and push your shoulder blades farther back. Hold your head between your arms, rather than letting it dangle, and press your heels downward.

- Your body will form an inverted V, with your backside at the point of the V. Hold this pose, just following your breath, for the next minute or two, feeling the stretch through your whole body. Notice any changes in your mental or physical state after this practice.

Happy Baby Pose

This pose can be comforting, relaxing, and restorative when you feel overwhelmed or frustrated by your performance before, during, or after a game.

- Lie down on your back. Take a few breaths, and on an exhale, draw your knees toward your chest.

- As you inhale, grab the outsides of your feet, opening your knees downward toward the sides of your torso and upward toward your armpits. Keep your ankles over your knees so that your shins are perpendicular to the floor.

- Flexing your heels, push your feet up as you pull your hands downward, keeping your shoulders as still as possible. Allow your spine to lengthen and stretch on the ground beneath you, with the base of your skull pulling upward, extending the stretch, and your tailbone pushing downward toward the floor.

- Very gently allow yourself to rock from side to side as you stretch and loosen your muscles. Remember to smile; you are a *happy* baby!

- Remain in this stretch for a minute or two, then release your feet back downward to the floor on an exhale, and rest. Notice any changes in your mental or physical state after this practice.

Eagle Pose

Yoga balancing poses like this one help boost coordination and concentration while building control and awareness of the smallest muscle movements.

- Stretch your arms forward, and cross your right arm above your left. Bend your elbows upward, twisting your arms so that your palms can grip each other as much as possible.

- Stand with your feet about shoulder- or hip-width apart (this is often closer than we think). Raise your left knee upward toward your chest. Bend your right knee and cross your left leg over your right, as high on your thigh as you can, hooking your left toes behind your right calf. Balance for a moment on your right foot.

- Raise your arms upward, and slowly lower the rest of your body down by bending your right knee, maintaining your balance the whole time. It can help to pick a spot on the ground or horizon to hold your eyes on. Maintain this pose for a few breaths or up to a minute.

- Stand, unwind, and repeat on the opposite side for the same length of time or number of breaths. Notice any changes in your mental or physical state after this practice.

Which of these poses did you find most helpful?

_____

_____

What did you notice before, during, and after the poses?

_____

_____

Did you find it easier to focus on your body than on your mind? Or was it harder?

_____

_____

47 putting on performances

Once you stop to think about it, you may be surprised to realize how often you are performing for groups that are not small or insignificant, from presentations in front of the class to plays and musical performances to athletic events.

The best preparation for any performance is practice. But what you might not know is that practice in your mind is often as helpful as actual practice with your body. Visualization meditations are helpful for going into a performance situation with minimal anxiety and maximum preparation, whether it is a musical performance, an athletic performance, or something else altogether.

Mindfulness Practice: The Maestro

- First, find a quiet place to relax, and get yourself comfortable in a position you can maintain for five or ten minutes. You can be sitting or lying down for this exercise. Begin by taking a few deep breaths and allowing your body and mind to just relax a bit.

- Imagine now that you are alone, perhaps in an empty concert hall or sports arena, or maybe somewhere else altogether, practicing whatever you will be performing soon. The seats are empty, and there is a light shining on you as you practice. You can hear the echoes of your own footsteps and feel the sensations of your hands on the ball, racquet, or instrument, even noticing the smells of wood or grass. You are the only person around, just there to practice and perfect your art. Soak up the atmosphere for a moment.

- When you feel ready, allow yourself to mentally practice the motions required. Visualize and rehearse all the physical movements you need to make as if you were actually making them. As you feel increasingly confident in your skills, you hear footsteps in the distance.

- Looking into the dark, you see a figure stepping into the light with you. It is your hero, your role model in your craft, the dream coach or teacher you've always admired. He or she approaches with a warm smile, and you introduce yourselves. The master teacher offers whatever guidance you need or want.

- You take a few minutes now to listen and practice together, movements in sync as you learn from your master. You visualize your movements reaching perfection, feel your body moving in a way that is just right. With a reminder that he or she is always there to help you, to offer advice or support, the master says it is time to depart. You can always hear your master's voice by listening deeply within your body and feel his or her presence close by.

- Take a moment to say thanks, perhaps in words or with a smile or nod, and just watch this person depart from the light, his or her voice still ringing in your mind, and the newly polished skills remembered in your body.

- And now, keeping these feelings with you, take a moment just to wiggle your toes and fingertips, allow your eyes to open, and come back into the room.

48 stage fright

Even for confident people, performing in front of a large audience can be unnerving. It is easy to worry about choking once we are onstage, in front of a class, or in the stadium performing. For the best performance, we want enough stress to give us energy, but not so much that it hinders our ability to think clearly. If we imagine stress levels ranging from one to ten, we want to be somewhere between six and eight.

What level does your anxiety tend to be before a big performance onstage?

_____

What do you usually do to bring it down when it's too high?

_____

_____

_____

In activity 28, you practiced progressive muscle relaxation, which is an excellent way to strengthen the mind-body connection and relax the body and mind. You might also remember experimenting with the feeling of making fists, and then letting go and allowing yourself to open. Before a big performance, you probably don't have time to lie down and flex each muscle group in turn, but you can take a moment to quickly move through the main muscle groups in your body to calm your whole system down to where it needs to be.

Mindful Practice: Mini Muscle Relaxation

- Take a moment to inhale deeply, shrug your shoulders, and then relax and let the shoulders drop. Feel the contrast between squeezing and releasing, before and after.

- Now ball your hands into fists, feeling the tension all the way from your fingers up your arms, and then just release, again allowing the relaxation to flow back into the muscles.

- Next, tighten the muscles in your stomach, hips, and buttocks. Just squeeze and release, feeling the tension drain away.

- Stretch your toes and flex your calves and then thighs for just a moment. Release and notice as the relaxation flows in, washing away the tension.

- Clench your jaw and neck (and if you are in private, you might want to squeeze your eyes shut tight at the same time), then just release.

- Take a few breaths now to notice the difference in your body.

- Take a deep breath, expand your chest, and walk confidently toward your performance.

Give this practice a try before your next performance.

49 driving

Many teens cannot wait for the opportunity to learn to drive. Finally reaching this exciting milestone, with the freedom it brings, is one of the best things about the teenage years. But for others, with the excitement comes anxiety, sometimes just reasonable concern, but sometimes escalating into avoidance of driving altogether.

I worked for a number of years with a young woman named Gina. She was a successful actor and singer, always one of the leads in the school play, with no anxiety or stage fright. She needed a summer job but never got around to applying, which drove her parents crazy. It wasn't anxiety, it wasn't procrastination, and it wasn't laziness. Finally, one evening in my office, she broke down. "It's the driving," she finally admitted through her tears. "I'm afraid of driving, and if I get a job I won't have any more excuses not to get my license."

Gina had never had a bad experience driving or even as a passenger. But still, the thought of driving terrified her. Part of it was the responsibility; she was worried she wouldn't be able to control the car and would hurt others or herself. She knew all the statistics about how safe driving actually was, and her parents had a car with side airbags, antilock brakes, and other safety devices, but still, she was afraid.

Gina and I had done some mindfulness practices in the past. We discussed the many benefits of bringing mindful awareness to driving, and together we came up with some ways to remain connected, relaxed, and still safe while driving.

Mindfulness Practice: Driving

- First, walk to the car mindfully, with the intention of being mindful for the drive.

- Bring your attention to each of the actions, sounds, and sensations involved in getting to and into the car.

- Once seated, spend some time behind the wheel without driving, just focusing on the sensations of your breath, of your hands on the wheel, of your feet on the pedals, and of your buttocks on the seat.

- Adjust the seat until you feel just right, alert but not strained.

- Adjust the mirrors, scanning your whole field of vision, from windshield ahead to mirrors on the side to behind you.

- Take a moment to notice how safe the car is—notice airbags, seatbelts, and everything else that can keep you and others safe.

- Now turn on the car, and just sit, feeling the vibrations and listening to the sounds of the engine.

- Visualize the drive to your destination—the roads, the turns, the easy parts and harder parts—and imagine staying calm through the whole thing.

- Once you are driving, deliberately bring your mindful attention to whatever you are doing by saying to yourself, *Now I'm going to take a left…now I'm going to put on the brake…now I'm going to put the car into reverse.* Whenever you reach a stop sign or stoplight, use the opportunity to quickly check in with your breath and body, and maybe take a relaxing deep breath.

- Finally, once you arrive, take a moment to acknowledge and even celebrate your success, just before gathering your things and getting out of the car.

To stay in the moment, it can help to deliberately not listen to music, but instead listen to the sounds of the car and feel the vibrations of the engine and bumps in the road. Some people prefer calming music. You can also just take the first five minutes of the drive in silence.

As you've learned to do during mindful walking, you can also use the drive to deliberately notice a few beautiful things along the way. Doing that will help your mind stay open and positive about the experience. Each time you notice something pretty on the drive, it can serve as another reminder to check in with your mind and body, while helping you enjoy the journey in the moment rather than focusing on the destination in the future.

Mindfulness not only keeps us calm but also makes us safer by slowing down our frustration with other drivers, keeping our impulsivity in check, decreasing our reaction times in dangerous scenarios, and overall, keeping us more alert.

50 panic attacks

Sometimes, all of our efforts to prevent anxiety by changing our external lives or trying to calm our internal states are not quite enough. Sometimes, we end up with the situation that many of us dread. Sometimes, no matter what we do, panic attacks still set in.

A panic attack does not mean that you're a failure or that you aren't trying hard enough. All it means is that your body just cannot take anymore and, like one in five other people in your life, you too experience panic.

As you may already realize, a panic attack ends and you will survive. Usually, it will be over within a few minutes, and you'll feel better afterward, even though you might feel exhausted. It is important that you not feel ashamed or angry at yourself, that you not beat yourself up about having a panic attack. People who have experienced a panic attack often live in fear of having another one, raising their overall anxiety, and making a recurrence more likely. This is exactly why it is important to practice mindfulness, relaxation, and other activities that reduce your baseline anxiety and stress on a regular basis, not just in moments of anxiety.

You might not even know if you have had or are experiencing a panic attack. Here are a few of the symptoms that many people experience:

- Chest pain (Many people think they are having a heart attack.)

- Difficulty breathing (It can also seem like an asthma attack.)

- Feeling out of control

- Feeling weak or faint

- Heart pounding (Many people worry that others can hear it because it seems so loud.)

- Hot or cold flashes

- Intense feelings of dread or that something terrible will happen

- Intense sweating

- Nausea or stomach cramping

- Shaking, shivering, or trembling

- Tingling in hands and feet

In the moment of a panic attack, it can be very difficult to access your mind's wisdom—to remember that the panic attach will end, that you are safe, and that you are not in danger. For that reason, it can also be helpful to have a list of people who know about your anxiety whom you can get in touch with when times get tough.

Whom can you reach out to in times of anxiety? Write down a few names here, including contact information, and keep a copy of the list on a separate sheet of paper, your phone, or your computer.

_____

_____

_____

_____

_____

_____

Mindfulness Practice: Let It RAIN

My friend Sara likes to say, "Mindfulness isn't about calming the storm; it is about finding the calm in the storm." Panic attacks are the hurricanes, tornadoes, and blizzards of anxiety all in one, and sunshine can look very far away. But every hurricane has an eye, the calm point at the center, and amid the turmoil, we can even welcome the rain with this practice, which many people use to help themselves through difficult situations like panic attacks.

- **R**ecognize what is happening. Recognition means identifying what is happening and knowing it for what it is. And if you have experienced it before, you have survived it, even if it was awful. Probably not the first time, but with practice, your thought process can become *Aha! This is a panic attack, nothing more, nothing less.* Just recognition can take away some of the power of the storm.

- **A**llow and accept. Allowing and even accepting a situation does not mean liking it; it means not denying reality or running away from it. It also means not judging yourself for what is happening. In the event of a panic attack, it means allowing your body to do what it does and waiting for the storm to pass. When was the last time you heard about someone successfully controlling a hurricane or other force of nature? There is a saying in psychotherapy: "What we resist persists."

- **I**nvestigate with kindness. What is the truth of this moment? It is not that you're in danger, but that your body and mind are trying to protect you, and they just happen to be overreacting. What is happening in your body? Do the sensations ebb and flow, or are they constant? Are your thoughts continuous and all negative, or are there spaces between them where you can find the calm? What are the fearful stories about? Whose voice is telling the story, who is listening to it, and do you have to believe it? Finally, is there something about this experience that needs your attention? Does your body, mind, or spirit need attending to in some way?

- **N**onidentify. This is a tricky one, the idea of nonidentification, but basically, it means: "Don't take it personally." It's not your fault, your feelings aren't facts, and your thoughts don't define who you are as a person.

When we actually practice RAIN, we come to find the calm in the storm and can rest there until it passes, even learning something from it. Although the description you just read is to help you with panic, using RAIN can be helpful at any time. It can help you become more aware as you go about your daily life. Earlier, you learned about STOP, and different times of day to use that acronym. You can try RAIN as a substitute for STOP at regular times during your busy day or week, or use it when you know you are walking into a situation that is going to challenge you or build into a storm.

51 making decisions

The challenge of living in a free country is that we are constantly faced with choices. Do I go to a small college or a big college? Date the jock or the honors student? One recent study found that there were more than four hundred types of toothpaste to choose from! Freedom of choice should be a good thing, and for most of us it is. But for some of us, decisions, big and small, can cause tremendous anxiety.

For those of us who get anxious when making a decision, a bit of mindfulness can go a long way toward easing the tension. Fear of making decisions is mostly about fear of making the *wrong* decision. It is the distortion that the wrong decision will lead to catastrophic consequences, and the right decision will lead to a perfect outcome—another example of black-and-white thinking. The reality is always somewhere in between, and once we accept that, we can start to move forward effectively.

By waiting and taking more time to decide, people who struggle with decision anxiety may find that no decision becomes a decision itself. Not taking action has its own consequences, and these can be worse than the consequences of one decision or the other.

A first-year college student named Tim came to my office about five years ago, telling me that his life was great except for one thing—he simply could not make decisions. As Tim was growing up, his parents had placed a lot of academic pressure on him to succeed and become a doctor, which may have been the source of some of his anxiety.

Tim's difficulty with decisions was profound. Not only could he not decide about classes or a career, he literally could not decide what to eat for lunch without serious stress. Eventually, his not taking action led to decisions being made for him, and he missed out on two internships and an opportunity to study abroad.

Mindfulness helped Tim see things more flexibly, accept what would come his way, and clearly see that *any* decision has pluses and minuses. He also began finding ways to bring his mind to a balanced place where he could most trust his decisions without looking backward or forward in regret or panic, without second-guessing himself.

In dialectical behavior therapy, a kind of psychotherapy, there are three states of mind:

- *Emotional mind* can involve a state of fear or even excitement. It is a passionate state that is important for enjoying life spontaneously and for survival, but not always the best one for making long-term decisions.

- *Rational mind* involves looking at the cold facts and making decisions analytically. It brings another useful way to make decisions, but can lead to a life without much fun or spontaneity.

- *Wise mind* is the area where our rational and emotional minds overlap. It is the state where we are most authentically ourselves and able to think, speak, and act in our most clear and thoughtful way. To make our best decisions, we want to be in wise mind.

What are some times when it can be helpful to be in rational mind?

_____

_____

What are some times when emotional mind is the best mind-set?

_____

_____

Think of some times when you've made a decision that you later regretted. Was there too much emotion or logic involved?

_____

_____

What are some times you have been in wise mind?

_____

_____

What activities or practices help you get into more of a wise-mind state?

_____

_____

_____

_____

Which of those could you imagine doing mindfully for the next week?

_____

_____

Choose one activity or practice to commit to. Circle it above and put a note in your calendar, or set an alarm on your phone to remind you. At the end of the week, review what you noticed, paying careful attention to all your senses.

Summing Up

Not everything that triggers our anxiety falls into a neat category. For many of us, anxiety lurks in unexpected and seemingly random places, but we can come to know when we are triggered, whether it is by driving, sports, or other unavoidable parts of adolescence. And sometimes, in spite of our best efforts and hard work, anxiety takes over, and waiting it out, rather than fighting, is the wisest course of action. There are certainly even more scenarios where anxiety can strike than could possibly fit in this book, but as you practice the different skills and discover what works for you, you can use what you learn for any situation, as you grow up, make more and more tough decisions, travel to college or go abroad, and eventually begin your career and family.

Take a moment now to reflect on the lessons, skills, and practices in this section.

Which activity did you relate to most?

_____

_____

What skills do you think you would be most likely to use in your daily life?

_____

_____

_____

Beyond the situations covered in this book, when else could you try some of the skills you have learned?

_____

_____

Which skills do you think you can try in the next week?

_____

_____

Put them in your calendar, and do them!

In the book *A Return to Love: Reflections on the Principles of "A Course in Miracles,"* author and lecturer Marianne Williamson writes:

> Our deepest fear is not that we are inadequate. Our deepest fear is that we are powerful beyond measure. It is our light, not our darkness, that most frightens us. We ask ourselves, who am I to be brilliant, gorgeous, talented, fabulous? Actually, who are you not to be?...And as we let our own light shine, we unconsciously give other people permission to do the same. As we are liberated from our own fear, our presence automatically liberates others.

Bringing It All Together

A friend of mine once described learning to be mindful this way:

> *I used to feel like I was living trapped in a closet with all my worries and thoughts stuffed inside with me. I couldn't breathe; I could hardly move! Now it's more like I'm living in an airplane hangar. Sure, some of the thoughts and worries are there, but they don't get in my way, and I don't bump into them unexpectedly because I can see where they are and avoid them.*

Hopefully this book has been useful to you in dealing with some of the most common forms of anxiety that you and millions of other adolescents face each day. By now you probably have a few strategies for staying calm at home, at school, in social situations, and elsewhere that you can use before, during, and after those moments when anxiety is most likely to strike.

We discussed formal meditation practices and short mindful moments. There are numerous activities you can do mindfully, from work to play, on a daily basis. There are also dozens, if not hundreds, of times a day for even the busiest people to do practices that take less than a minute; for example, STOP, RAIN, 7/11 Breathing, Harnessing the Four Elements, and CALM.

Mindfulness does not have to be difficult, time consuming, or strange. Here are several times when you might be able to grab a moment of mindfulness during the day:

- Waking up in the morning, before you check your phone

- Whenever you hear the doorbell ring or phone chime with a new message

- Whenever you hear microwave or kitchen timers go off

- Walking up the first few steps of a staircase

- Each time you reach for a doorknob or a sink faucet

- When you hear the telephone ring

- Waiting for water to boil or your food to cook

- Before or after you turn on a light switch or press an elevator button

- Waiting for your printer to print your homework (always a happy time of day!)

- Waiting for your computer or video game system to load

- Walking to school or at points along the way (for example, stoplights, crossings, or corners)

- Standing in line

- Waiting for your sibling to get out of the bathroom in the morning

I hope you have seen how simple and effective mindfulness can be in everyday life. May this book help you live a life free of unnecessary anxiety and stress.

I leave you with this poem about stillness and fear:

I go among trees and sit still.
All my stirring becomes quiet
around me like circles on water.
My tasks lie in their places
where I left them, asleep like cattle.

Then what is afraid of me comes
and lives a while in my sight.
What it fears in me leaves me,
and the fear of me leaves it.
It sings, and I hear its song.

Then what I am afraid of comes.
I live for a while in its sight.
What I fear in it leaves it,
and the fear of it leaves me.
It sings, and I hear its song.

After days of labor,
mute in my consternations,
I hear my song at last,
and I sing it. As we sing,
the day turns, the trees move.

—Wendell Berry, "Go Among Trees"

Christopher Willard, PsyD, is a psychologist and learning specialist in the Boston area who specializes in working with adolescents and young adults in his private practice at Tufts University. He regularly consults schools, clinics, and other institutions, and teaches workshops across the US and around the world. His website can be found at drchristopherwillard.com.

FROM OUR PUBLISHER—

As the publisher at New Harbinger and a clinical psychologist since 1978, I know that emotional problems are best helped with evidence-based therapies. These are the treatments derived from scientific research (randomized controlled trials) that show what works. Whether these treatments are delivered by trained clinicians or found in a self-help book, they are designed to provide you with proven strategies to overcome your problem.

Therapies that aren't evidence-based—whether offered by clinicians or in books—are much less likely to help. In fact, therapies that aren't guided by science may not help you at all. That's why this New Harbinger book is based on scientific evidence that the treatment can relieve emotional pain.

This is important: if this book isn't enough, and you need the help of a skilled therapist, use the following resource to find a clinician trained in the evidence-based protocols appropriate for your problem. And if you need more support— a community that understands what you're going through and can show you ways to cope—a resource for that is provided below, as well.

Real help is available for the problems you have been struggling with. The skills you can learn from evidence-based therapies will change your life.

Matthew McKay, PhD
Publisher, New Harbinger Publications

If you need a therapist, the following organization can help you find a therapist trained in cognitive behavioral therapy (CBT).

The Association for Behavioral & Cognitive Therapies (ABCT) Find-a-Therapist service offers a list of therapists schooled in CBT techniques. Therapists listed are licensed professionals who have met the membership requirements of ABCT and who have chosen to appear in the directory.

Please visit www.abct.org and click on *Find a Therapist*.

For additional support for patients, family, and friends, please contact the following:

Anxiety and Depression Association of American (ADAA)
please visit www.adaa.org

More Instant Help Books for Teens

An Imprint of New Harbinger Publications

**THE ANXIETY WORKBOOK
FOR TEENS**

Activities to Help You Deal
with Anxiety & Worry

ISBN: 978-1572246034 / US $14.95
Also available as an e-book

**GET OUT OF YOUR MIND &
INTO YOUR LIFE FOR TEENS**

A Guide to Living an
Extraordinary Life

ISBN: 978-1608821938 / US $15.95
Also available as an e-book

**THE ANGER WORKBOOK
FOR TEENS**

Activities to Help You Deal with
Anger & Frustration

ISBN: 978-1572246997 / US $15.95
Also available as an e-book

COPING WITH CLIQUES

A Workbook to Help Girls Deal
with Gossip, Put-Downs, Bullying
& Other Mean Behavior

ISBN: 978-1572246133 / US $16.95
Also available as an e-book

**DON'T LET YOUR
EMOTIONS RUN
YOUR LIFE FOR TEENS**

Dialectical Behavior Therapy Skills
for Helping You Manage Mood
Swings, Control Angry Outbursts
& Get Along with Others

ISBN: 978-1572248830 / US $16.95
Also available as an e-book

**THINK CONFIDENT,
BE CONFIDENT FOR TEENS**

A Cognitive Therapy Guide to
Overcoming Self-Doubt & Creating
Unshakable Self-Esteem

ISBN: 978-1608821136 / US $16.95
Also available as an e-book

newharbingerpublications
1-800-748-6273 / newharbinger.com

(VISA, MC, AMEX / prices subject to change without notice)

 Like us on Facebook   Follow us on Twitter @newharbinger.com

Don't miss out on new books in the subjects that interest you.
Sign up for our **Book Alerts** at **newharbinger.com/bookalerts**